In case of loss, please return to:

_____
_____
_____
_____

As a reward: $ _____

EXCHANGE
THE

TIRED OF LIVING THE CHRISTIAN LIFE ON YOUR OWN?

Joel Engle

Published by LifeWay Press®
© 2007 Joel Engle

ISBN: 1-4158-5270-7
005035511

Dewey Decimal Classification Number: 248.84
Subject Heading: CHRISTIAN LIFE\BIBLE. N.T. ROMANS-STUDY

Printed in the United States of America

Leadership and Adult Publishing
LifeWay Church Resources
One LifeWay Plaza
Nashville, Tennessee 37234-0175

We believe the Bible has God for its author; salvation for its end; and truth, without any mixture of error, for its matter and that all Scripture is totally true and trustworthy. The 2000 statement of The Baptist Faith and Message is our doctrinal guideline.

CONTENTS

JOEL ENGLE

Joel Engle is a worship leader, songwriter, and musician who through his gifts of communication inspires students, young adults, and churches to a deeper, more fulfilling relationship with Jesus.

Joel's personal experiences have played an enormous role in the formation of who he is as a Christian leader, believer, husband, and father. Walking through the tragic circumstances surrounding the abandonment of his father, the death of his mother, the loss of his grandparents, and eventually his time in foster care have profoundly influenced his view of life with Christ.

Today Joel communicates a message of hope for those who have experienced similar loss as well as those who believe there is more to life than what they are experiencing. Through his music, speaking and writing Joel imparts the truth of what Christ is in him—and what Christ can be in everyone.

Today Joel makes his home in Texas with his wife, Valerie, and their children. Find out more about the ministry of Joel Engle at *www.joelengle.com*.

MEET THE AUTHOR

EXCHANGE
THE
TIRED OF LIVING THE CHRISTIAN LIFE ON YOUR OWN?

Entering the Exchange

THE APPLE TREES

IMAGINE YOU ARE WALKING THROUGH AN APPLE ORCHARD IN EARLY SPRING. THE
DELICATE FRAGRANCE OF THE APPLE BLOSSOM PERFUMES THE COOL MORNING AIR.
THAT FLORAL SCENT IS ENOUGH TO TRIGGER MEMORY; YOU CLEARLY RECALL THE
SWEET JUICY CHOMP OF THE RED DELICIOUS.

SUDDENLY, YOU STOP. IN THE HEIGHTENED SENSORY MOMENT, YOUR EARS GROW VERY
SENSITIVE. THEY PROBE FOR ANY SOUND. WHAT DO YOU HEAR? NOTHING. TOTAL SILENCE.

AN APPLE (OR ANY KIND OF FRUIT) TREE IS ONE OF THE MOST MARVELOUS
MYSTERIES IN THE WORLD. NO ONE CAN QUITE FATHOM THE EXQUISITE PERFECTION
OF PHOTOSYNTHESIS; SOIL, SUNLIGHT, WATER, AND TEMPERATURES FLOW TOGETHER
INTO A WONDROUS HARMONY OF CREATION. THE RESULT OF THIS SPLENDID FUSION
IS THAT THE BLOSSOMS ON THE TREE SLOWLY MORPH INTO APPLES.

Incredibly, despite the great industry going on in those trees, they do it all effortlessly and silently. They don't work at it or have any form of apple anxiety. It is simply their nature to produce apples.

Apples happen naturally. Now, imagine another apple orchard. As you walk into it, you hear a low mumbling hum. At first, you wonder if insects are swarming the orchard. But as you stop near a particular apple tree, you hear a very distinct grunting. What? You move your head close to the branches. The grunting sound is coming from the tree itself! Yes, the apple tree is panting, then bearing down, and finally emitting a long agonizing growl.

You see, these are "Christian" apple trees. They've been taught that bearing apples is almost impossible, requires great straining, and is a "skill" which can easily be lost.

THE LIE
Christian culture (especially in America) has created an outrageous, dangerous, and deadly lie about what life with Jesus is like. That lie goes something like this: our Father God is an elderly, somewhat senile, and angry Presence who lives in the swirling dark storm clouds.

True to His gloomy nature, He devised a sad, loveless, cruel and frankly impossible life for the "earthlings." He gave very specific and demanding rules for how to live that life. But He knew they would fail. He prepared a very hot and sulfuric lake of fire called "hell" for all those who (so naturally and inevitably) fail.
The lie goes on to explain what many call the "good news." The "good news," according to

the lie, is that God finally realized that He must do something to give a legal way of escape from this very heavy and unhappy way of life. So His solution (which theologians try to explain, but we still don't quite understand) was to direct His Son Jesus to die for the sins of the people. As the obedient Son, Jesus did die; He paid the cost for our sin so that the people might—*might*—be saved.

So He died. The result of that death, at least in this cultural lie, is that humans can squeak into heaven by the skin of their teeth, if they can work hard enough to live up to Jesus' sacrifice. See, in this lie, even though Jesus died to deliver *new* life, *new* rules, and the *new* era of the Kingdom, the same harshness of the *old* still prevails. Despite the "New Testament" freshness, that lie still insists on an earthbound, grueling, human-centered scheme. That story ignores or denies the power of the superior life—that Jesus came to help the humans and has the power to do so. In the lie, Father God still required the very best and very strenuous efforts of people. He was still very severe and demanding.

The only difference is that, now, the people had to deal with the Son. If they didn't remember and keep all the new covenant rules and didn't try hard enough to be holy—through prayer and fasting, reading the Bible, and going to church a lot—they were still going to fall into that fiery furnace when they died.

THE EXCHANGE
Perhaps you, too, have some misconceptions about Christianity that come from your culture rather than your Bible. So what is the truth?

Just as apple trees don't try to "have an apple," those who follow Christ aren't meant to will themselves to "live a Christian life." The main reason? No one can do it. Yes, you read that correctly. No one can live the Christian life.

One of the best kept secrets of the true Christian life is that Jesus actually lives His life through us; He does it all. He is the fullness of life and that superior life surges through our heart, our relationships, our attitudes, and our behaviors. That higher quality of life makes all things new. He doesn't just require something; He also provides what He requires.

Now, *that* is good news! Yes, of course, when He died He fulfilled the eternal requirements of a just God. But, in so doing, He took our life and nature onto Himself, nailed it to that tree, and then poured out His life so that we could all share it. Everyone who hears and responds is invited to cash in their life for His. The cross was the scene of a life exchange.

So there it is. That is the exchange. It's the essence of classical Christian faith. Yet, it has become covered over by the rubble of several centuries of Christian culture. I think three chapters of the Bible—Romans 6, 7, and 8—capture the simple, but transforming, reality of the Christian life better than anything else ever written. The Apostle Paul knocked the theological ball out of the park and on out of the earth's atmosphere.

Those Scriptures are a waterfall of revelation; they cascade in a thunderous roar from Heaven to earth. But so few people have ever heard these truths, much less embraced them as the right way to live. So strap yourself in. I want to pass on what the Lord has used to radically reorder my entire life. It was resurrection power to me. I know it can be to you also.

TRUTH YOU CAN TRUST

A very wise man once said that truth which has not been lived in is stolen truth. In other words, if truth has not been broiled in the furnace of your own challenges and adversities, it will not nourish or sustain anyone else. You always know when you hear truth that was lived in; it carries that unmistakable ping of reality. It has become truth you can trust.

I know the exchange is true because it has been lived in my own life. I'll give you the details later, but I grew up so lonely, fearful, and unhappy that I was a seriously damaged kid. At 11 years old, I had no one to care for me. As an angry loner, I quickly decided that it all depended on me. Loneliness and anxiety can be so overwhelming that they suck all of life into a dark, bottomless, swirling void.

What I'm writing is not some cool theory. The truth in this book has been broiled, fried, and electrified in the laboratory of my own life. When I found the faith to just "give up" to God, I found that the kind and generous Savior was ready to move into my life and live through me. He made me a deal I couldn't refuse: "Give Me your life, and I'll give you Mine." Now my story is His story. He exchanged life with me.
In the exchange, you'll find a way of life which flows out as naturally as apples stream from the branches of the tree. The result is a continuing harvest of sweetness, flavor, and full-throttle joy.

HOW TO READ THIS BOOK

Finally, I want to explain the idea of this book and give some suggestions on how to read it. I wholeheartedly believe the truth of the apple tree. That tree is part of a larger inter-related dynamic of creation. There is nothing tentative or fragile about that synergistic process. As I've explained, all of that happens naturally and effortlessly. Apples appear because of the inherent nature of the tree as part of that living cycle.

That is the precise principle that Jesus taught when He wrote that He is the true vine and His disciples are the branches. The surging power of life is in Him, and that power flows out through all those who are the branches of the Vine. That is Jesus' explanation of the exchange (you'll find it in John 15).

Either you accept the principle of the apple tree or you don't, but everything past this point in the book builds from that orchard. If you do accept this truth, then what is written in the pages of this book can bring you closer to maturity in your walk with Christ.

Also, my writing style is probably somewhat like that of a basketball coach. Like a coach, I am primarily concerned with equipping you to reach your full potential. I see it as my job to drive and help you on your way to maturity as followers of Christ. Further, I won't treat you like infants; I am direct and use words like *should* and *must* and *stop* and *no*. I tell you that you may "have to" do some things. I want you to grow up.

Know also that this book is meant to be read, put down, and then read again. There are so many profound thoughts throughout Romans 6,7 and 8 that you may want to take some time and marinate in them for a while. You can read it in large chunks like any other book, but it is also designed to be read as quick cuts—maybe as you ride the bus, wait in line at the airport, wait for your friends at Starbucks, or sit in the beauty or barber chair. You see, I'm a musician; I tend to think of CD or MP3 "cuts." You can listen to the whole CD or you can listen to one cut at a time as you wait in the drive-up lane at the bank.

Finally, this is a "living" book. New chapters are being written by you in the rhythm of your own life. You will touch and experience dimensions of the exchange that I have never considered.

Please tell me your stories. I'm serious; I want to know how you touch the exchange, what it means to you, how it changes your world and makes all things new. I'm interested in your setbacks as well as your successes. You can email me at *joel@joelengle.com*.

May God bless you and open your heart and mind as you step into the waters of *The Exchange*.

SESSION 1

Exchanging Perspective

WE EXCHANGE a lot of things in life: shirts, CDs, cars, even people. Most of the time, we do so because we have become convinced that we can trade in what we currently have for something better. This spiritual exchange is no different.

It's time to stop "doing our best for God" and realize that the sinful nature we inherited from Adam has died through the sacrifice of Jesus. Now His person lives within us. Just as wind will catch the sails of a schooner and pull it through the waves, we are now filled up with the power of that superior life. We can put the oars away. No need to row when the wind is full in the sails.

This is what I mean by "the exchange." We exchange our inability for Christ's perfect ability. If we try to live our lives in our human strength, then we are living from the power of our own rowing. The only possible outcome is an ineffective life, being continually exhausted by the effort and the inevitable defeat. After all, rowing is hard work.

EXCHANGING PERSPECTIVE

ROMANS 6:1-14

DAMAGED

I will never forget the day of my mom's funeral.

I was 11 years old. It was a cool morning, typical of the weeks before the suffocating blanket of summer heat falls across north central Oklahoma. I still remember how the big, black limousine crunched the gravel of our driveway as it rolled to a stop. I remember Grandma and Grandpa dressed in their Sunday clothes as they climbed into the limo.

We arrived at Buckley's Funeral home in downtown Wetumka. I was the first to get out of the car. A deep sense of dread came over me as I got ready to see my mom for the last time.

The moment was surreal, like a dream that played out in slow motion. I walked up the stairs to the door of the funeral home. Right there, through the plate-glass window of the front door, I saw the profile of my mom's face as she lay in the casket. I lost my breath and turned away. After a few minutes, I slowly walked back up the steps, through the door, and slipped into the waiting room. I didn't want to go into the viewing room. Not yet.

Watch the video segment "The Bottom Line from Dr. Frank" when your group meets to discuss this session. It will help you understand what this "exchange" is about.

Grandma put her arm around me and said that I really needed to see my Mom for the last time. Reluctantly, I walked into the room. My mouth was dry, my heart pounding. The flowered mortuary odor seemed to carry the weird and scary essence of death. I walked toward her beautiful face in the purple light of the open casket. The body didn't look like my Mom.

"They have really made her look beautiful," Grandma whispered. Those were empty words to an 11-year-old boy. To me, there was no one in the casket. My mom was gone. Her high pitched laugh that made everyone else laugh was forever silent. Her voice would never be heard again. Her warm touch was now cold. Her sense of humor would never again make life so funny. She was simply not there, and my life seemed to be fading away too.

This was the second most terrible day of my life. The worst one was five days earlier when the doctor told me that Mom had only 30 minutes to live. So the two most horrible days of my life happened within one week. The day my Mom died and the day of her funeral have colored every day of the rest of my life.

Session 1 **The Exchange**

For what seemed to be a very long time, I carried a deep and endless void in my life. I suffered just about every psychological trauma you can imagine: fear, anger, rage, and overpowering loneliness. Depression, rejection, boredom, cynicism, and suicidal thoughts are roads that I have traveled often and know intimately.

I never knew my father, so I had to grow up without him or Mom. Naturally, I saw a lot of psychiatrists and therapists. Sometimes they helped, but more often than not, I immediately returned to an empty life. Living in Christian homes, I attended church and read my Bible faithfully, and I still could not find joy, peace, and hope. Death can do that to you.

ESCAPE FROM DEATH

You don't have to be paralyzed by fear, anxiety, and guilt. All of those things are little tentacles emerging and twisting out of the power of death. That power is the real issue behind the smaller emotions.

I lived in the shadow of death from the time (and probably even before) I was 11 years old. That enslavement to death took me into a dark and despairing whirlpool of fear and depression.

Living like that is a failure to realize that Jesus has dealt with the real issue. He ruined death, irreparably breaking it. When He died on the cross, He gutted death of its power. I really like the way the writer of Hebrews says it: **"Now since the children have flesh and blood in common, He also shared in these, so that through His death He might destroy the one holding the power of death—that is, the Devil—and free those who were held in slavery all their lives by the fear of death" (Hebrews 2:14-15).**

Because He appeared, I (and everyone else who follows Him) moved from living in the shadow of death to living in the shadow of His cross. That's why I wrote the song "Shadow of Your Cross." Consider these lyrics:

> *You chose the road of pain*
> *You walked the hills of all my shame, all my shame*
> *In the shadow of Your cross I will live for all my days*
> *How could I forget the price You paid.*

In dying on the cross and exchanging His life for our shame, Jesus brought freedom. Jesus didn't say that conferences, churches, worship CDs, books, and other religious stuff would set you free from the pain of an empty heart. Jesus said that He would set you free.

Listen to "The Shadow of Your Cross" from your *Exchange* playlist. Get a copy of the playlist from your group leader or at *www. threadsmedia.com/media.*

Now, you might say, "OK, Joel, I am a Christian. But if Jesus has set me free from the power of death, why do I feel so fearful and empty and bored with life?" Good question. I believe there are answers to this and many other questions, but it is so simple that many miss it. We think it just has to be more complicated and more difficult than it is.

Here it is: Christ is our life—literally. Through Him and His Word, He has given us everything we need in order to walk in freedom. *He sets us free*. He does that by removing the dead corpse of our old, sin-infested nature and giving us His character, confidence, courage, strength, peace, and joy.

That's it. All we have to do is give up our old self. Let Him haul it away. When He carts our old life away, the snarling threats of death are in that cart too. We exchange our life for His. The Apostle Paul describes the ins and outs of how that happens in the book of Romans.

"For I am not ashamed of the gospel, because it is God's power for salvation to everyone who believes, first to the Jew, and also to the Greek" (Romans 1:16).

This verse is part of what I love about Paul. Right up front he announces wonderful news. No problem statement to get our attention. He tells you immediately that anyone who wants the power of God can have it.

Paul doesn't lead with the bad news. Before he even looks at the sin problem, he essentially tells us that Jesus has already won. Paul leads his great book with a laser beam of hope. Further, this hope is not just for when we die; it is for every moment of our lives as well as eternity..

How do I get through this life on earth? How do I deal with the stress of trying to find my place in society? How do I deal with the nagging feeling of emptiness and meaninglessness that we all struggle with? How do I get through a difficult relationship?

Life in Christ empowers us for all these real issues. He is our hope for this life as well as when we die.

> For you, what are the implications for life with Christ in the present?

> What does an abundant life look like to you?

EARTH, WE HAVE A PROBLEM

After Paul has established that our hope is firmly fixed and secure, he essentially says, "OK, people, now let's face reality; the whole earth has a sin problem." Starting with Romans 1:18, Paul walks us through some pretty nasty evidence of sin and its corruption of the earth and society. And, I might add, he gives us a clear warning about the coming wrath of God against all sin.

Of course, we all know that sin is rampant in our world. We see it on CNN, hear it on the radio, and read about it every day. Wars, serial killers, drugs, crime, divorce, lying, and every other form of sin surges back and forth throughout our world.

So, what is God doing about the problem of sin? That's a fair question. If God is truly good and just, then doesn't He have to punish evil? If God is just, then why hasn't He wiped out all those who sin just like He did in the days of Noah? After all, a just legal system on this earth will assign appropriate punishments for crimes. If the wages of sin really is death (Romans 3:23), then why are we still here? Why are sinners not punished by a holy God as they are in the justice systems of modern society?

God, being rich in infinite wisdom, had a plan that began before the foundation of the world (Revelation 13:8). He sent His only son, Jesus Christ, to stand in our place and take our punishment upon Himself. So, the proper punishment for our sin wasn't overlooked or ignored by God. Instead, incredibly, He paid it Himself. The Father God marked our just punishment PAID IN FULL by the Son's work on the cross. In the legal system of most civilized societies, the *offender* pays the price, but in the infinite wisdom of God, the *Offended* has already paid the price.

I know this cuts across our independence and pride, but our problem runs way deeper than some minor behavioral infractions. You see, Adam and Eve are not mythical figures; they were real people created by God to enjoy intimate fellowship with Him.

Instead of choosing a love relationship with God, Adam and Eve chose sin (Don't judge them too hard; you and I wouldn't have done any better). Here's the really tough part: When they chose sin, they chose for all of us. The whole human race became separated from God. Because of Adam and Eve's disobedience, all of humanity is born with a sinful nature that expresses itself in rebellion against God. It is in our nature to sin.

If you think about all of the wars, murders, and bad motives that have floated within the heart of humanity from the beginning of time, you realize the tremendous damage that sin has imposed on the world from the very start of human existence. It makes you wonder why God would ever let anyone into His Heaven, the place of eternal fellowship with Himself. He could have left us in the vicious jaws of death, and He would have been totally justified in doing so. Instead, out of His infinite love, He sent Jesus to pay the price for our sin. That is the true yardstick for measuring love.

Before we can go any further, I must ask you this question: Have *you*—yes, you—experienced the life-exchange that Jesus offers? Are you still trying to do it all yourself? Are you trying so hard to measure up to God by your own human effort? Maybe you have never even thought about a relationship with God before.

It doesn't matter where you have been or what you have done in your life; the exchange is available to "whosoever will." Ask God to give you the gift of faith to trust what Jesus did for you by taking your sin upon Himself.

> **How has your experience of God's love been influenced by your experience of love on earth?**

> **Does God like you?**

REAL GRACE

I have to be honest with you; I struggled with the idea that a holy and good God could ever love someone like me. It was just too good to be true. Maybe it's because I was orphaned at such a young age, but the very idea of being totally forgiven and loved by the awesome God of creation and Ruler of the whole universe seemed like an *Oh-that's-nice* thought. It couldn't be real.

Yet the Bible is very clear about this: God loves us—period.

The absolute love and acceptance of God scares a lot of people today. Maybe it's because something in our makeup wants a part of the process which we can control. In other words, we want to have a role in our acceptance. That's what gives birth to legalism. If we can just know the rules around here, then we can try to keep them and, therefore, have a legal basis for acceptance.

Maybe it's because the idea of total forgiveness and unconditional grace seems to give license to live in bad, unchristian ways. If we're forgiven and under grace, why not just blow off the discipline and diligence it takes to live a purposeful life, right?

Session 1 **The Exchange**

"What should we say then? Should we continue in sin in order that grace may multiply? Absolutely not! How can we who died to sin still live in it?" (Romans 6:1-2).

Taking the grace of God lightly is an insult to God Himself. We need to remember that what was bought at such profound expense will not be ignored by our Lord. He knows how to deal with us if we abuse His grace. In fact, His discipline is a sign of His love and fatherhood.

To think His forgiveness is a license to sin is to be ignorant of the nature of grace. Paul knew, and declared: "We died to sin; how can we live in it any longer?" In other words, through the cross we have died to our sin heritage and been brought into a new family. We now have a Father Who knows how to raise His kids through loving, character-forming, discipline.

ADOPTION

Speaking of fatherhood, child psychologists know that the abandonment of a child by his parents, either by death or by choice, is one of the most damaging things possible. Some people never overcome it. It not only means that you've been rejected, but that you've also been severed from your own lineage.

When the power of death entered the world through Adam and Eve, a spirit of abandonment became engraved on the hearts and minds of their descendents. *We were cut off from our own familial lineage in God.* That alienation is a prime driver in depression and suicide. Even if one doesn't believe in God, he or she cannot cope with the *detachment* from the divine Parent. It's brutal.

That's why my adoption by the Engle family is one of the greatest evidences of God's fatherhood in my life. Being adopted was a very big deal because I was 16 years old when it happened. I mean, people adopt cute little cuddly babies, not teenagers with big problems and zits. They want a life they can nurture and mold, not a goofy, super-hyper adolescent.

But it happened; the Engle family adopted me, took me into their Garber, Oklahoma, home, and treated me as one of their own from the beginning. One Christmas at home, as we gathered around the Christmas tree to open presents, my sister Nancy asked if she could first say something to the whole family.

Get in on the discussion. Listen to the audio file "What Is the Essence of Christianity?" as you study this session. It will come via email from your group leader.

She looked at me, tears streaming down her face, and said, "Joel, I know you have been with us for a while, but I can't remember a single Christmas when you were not a part of our family!" I was 16 before I came to the Engle family, yet she couldn't remember a time without me as her brother. *That's what adoption means.*

That is why those who are unwilling to accept God's total forgiveness are missing the point. They live like they have to constantly remind God they are good kids, and they resent those who seem to live without that insecurity. That viewpoint completely neglects the true power and absolute finality of adoption.

> **How has your upbringing influenced your view of God as father?**

> **Has there ever been a point in your life that you took grace for granted?**

THE POWER OF BAPTISM

I will never forget my childhood pastor, Dr. Reed Lynn at First Baptist Church Wetumka, Oklahoma. We played ping-pong, went to football games, and did other things which fathers and sons do. I have a lot of good memories of him as my pastor.

He baptized me when I was 14 years old. I remember that the water was cold (someone said the heater was broken). In fact, Pastor Lynn had on some kind of weird rubber jumpsuit.

As we stood in that frigid tank, his deep, booming voice asked me, in front of the entire church congregation, if I professed Jesus Christ as my Savior. Just then, I slipped under the water before I was ready! Gravity and a slippery bottom dunked me. His voice announcing ". . . buried with Him in baptism" morphed into water flooding my ear canals. Then, as I was pulled up out of the water of that small baptistery, I heard the words, "raised to walk in newness of life." Then everybody clapped. But I never knew what those words really meant until I read Romans 6:3-4.

"Or are you unaware that all of us who were baptized into Christ Jesus were baptized into His death? Therefore we were buried with Him by baptism into death, in order that, just as Christ was raised from the dead by the glory of the Father, so we too may walk in a new way of life" (Romans 6:3-4).

In our spiritual baptism, we are buried and then resurrected with Christ. The same resurrection power which raised Jesus from the dead also raises us from death. Because of what Jesus did on the cross, we have now been united with Christ in His death. That means our old nature of sin has been killed and the corpse has been

Session 1 **The Exchange**

hauled away. As R. C. Sproul wrote, "The death sentence was pronounced upon my old nature . . . My sin was put to death on the cross of Jesus Christ . . ."[1]

Not only that, but we have now been united with Christ in His life. The same supernatural power that literally raised Jesus from the dead has raised every Christian from death to the joy of being alive in Christ. The moment we met Christ we had a spiritual extreme makeover.

Perhaps more significantly, our spiritual baptism cuts us off from our sin legacy and weaves us into God's family. We enter a brand-new life. Some Bible teachers claim the way to success in the Christian life is through a self-reliant bootstraps model of empowerment.

But through the power of Christ surging through us, we have all we need to experience the freedom for which God went to such great lengths to give. You can't have a changed live until you have an exchanged life.

> In your opinion up to this point, what is the place of effort in the Christian life?

> Have you ever felt like God was disappointed in your level of effort?

DUAL CITIZENSHIP

Let's face it; those who have been adopted into God's family live a very strange life. We are citizens of Heaven, but we don't live there. We still hang out in the mud and odors and conflict and sensuality of earth.

Jesus described that dichotomy well in speaking to the Pharisees: **"You are from below . . . I am from above. You are of this world; I am not of this world" (John 8:23).** As long as we live on earth, we can never be fully at home on earth and we can never fully escape the pull of its environment.

Our identity should be firmly rooted in Christ. But the glitz of earth continually sings its "siren song" to us. That song distracts us from our true identity, causing us to transfer our sense of who we are to earthly status symbols.

At that point, identity becomes entangled with what kind of car you drive, where you live, how much money you make, and how your appearance compares with celebrities. It seems that, on earth, empty status symbols have come to mean everything.

"For if we have been joined with Him in the likeness of His death, we will certainly also be in the likeness of His resurrection. For we know that our old self was crucified with Him in order that sin's dominion over the body may be abolished, so that we may no longer be enslaved to sin, since a person who has died is freed from sin's claims" (Romans 6:5-7).

By pressing into our identity and union with Christ and His death we begin to experience the freedom of knowing who we really are. As we do, we become more aware that our identity in Him is far more significant than anything the earth can offer. From the vantage point of our new identity, we can see that our earth-life was crucified and buried with Him. Because it is gone, we can escape our slavery to sin.

LORD OF THE RING

Even though we have an escape route from sin, there is still a powerful pull from the earth. It makes the needle of our moral compass spin wildly. In those moments of vertigo, we tend to reach out for more control of our lives and circumstances. We try to install ourselves as Lord of our own little universe.

Author Bill Gillham wrote, "When you showed up on planet earth in a little earthsuit two feet long, you drew a circle around yourself and declared, 'I am Lord of the Ring!' Oh you were willing to let God run the universe, but your attitude was 'I am god of all the turf inside this circle'".[2] We all, in various times and ways, become Lord of the Ring, totally obsessed with ourselves and controlled by sin.

When you met Christ, you were united with Him in His resurrection. What does that mean? It means that your old life died, but through Christ, you now have a new nature that loves God and desires to honor Him in every way. You have a new, sin-free, spiritual identity, and we have it right now. Francis Schaeffer wrote: "It is not just that we are dead to certain things, but we are to love God, we are to be alive to him, we are to be in communion with him, *in this present moment in history*".[3]

Imagine: we are now united with Christ. We are literally *in* Him, and at the same time, He is literally in us. Christ lives in our hearts. Our identity has been changed. We were once united with sin and death, and now we are united with Christ our life. It is time we begin to live like it; it's time to step down as Lord of the Ring!

We no longer have no right to live life on our own terms. Never again. We no longer belong to ourselves. Our Father simply does not extend permission for us to slip out of His house in order to indulge sin in the gutters of earth. To do so is to violate our relationship with the Head of our new family.

Session 1 **The Exchange**

We are alive; therefore, we are free to remain in His palace and to live in unbroken fellowship with Father God.

If we slip away and fall into sin, His door and His heart remain open. All we have to do is go back home; He will receive us with open arms. God doesn't hold our sins against us. But at some point we have to grow up. Mature and sane people do not walk away from the exquisite beauty and profound excellence of the castle to go sleep in the gutter and eat worms. This is not *normal*.

> What role does faith play in your day to day choices of sin or righteousness?

> What do you think God's opinion is of you when you "leave His house" for other pleasures?

CHOOSE LIFE

By the way, I do know, by personal experience, what it is to walk away from the palace and Father. When I met Jesus Christ for the first time, I really desired to live for Him with all my heart. I had a new nature and a new identity in Christ. I loved it, but didn't truly understand it. Despite my promising start in faith, it was not long before the feelings wore off and I drifted back to my old habits.

Was I really a Christian? Of course I was, but I was not mature. The formation process was not finished. Nobody told me that Christ had finished His redemption work, that my old nature was dead. Had I known that, I could have applied that death more effectively. Yes, I could have *"applied* death"; Paul wrote in Romans 6:11, **"*consider* yourselves to be dead to sin, but alive to God in Christ Jesus" (emphasis added).**

But because I didn't know that, I had some sinful patterns that were heavily influencing my life. I just didn't understand the power in Christ to live above those things. I really thought it was up to me, in my own power, to live for God.

So I tried and failed, tried and failed, and tried and failed once again. When I was about 23, I just said, "Forget this." I checked out; I stopped seeking God. I thought I could never please Him The pain of my childhood caught up with me and began to take a serious toll on me and those closest to me. Looking back and knowing what I know now, I am amazed (and grateful!) that I never turned to drugs, alcohol, or a gun to kill the pain. Clearly, the grip of His grace would not let me go.

At that point, however, I just kept sinking deeper in despair. I agonized over how I could be a Christian and still suffer such anguishing internal pain. Then one day, revelation from the Holy Spirit hit me like a bag of bricks. The Joel Engle that was so wounded and angry at the world had died when I put my trust in Christ at age 14. I just didn't know how to walk out that "death."

And then, through the newly discovered power of Jesus Christ, a new Joel Engle was resurrected! And, the "new man" was free from the anger and rebellion against God and could live in the joy and presence of God forever. I discovered a treasure: *the power to choose.*

Moses addressed the people of Israel one day: **"I call heaven and earth as witnesses against you today that I have set before you life and death, blessing and curse. *Choose life* so that you and your descendants may live" (Deuteronomy 30:19, emphasis added).**

.

Apparently, God gives us the power to choose life. You can choose life or you can choose death. Leaving the house of God to go live in a cardboard box is a choice. Staying warm and cozy inside the House of God is also a choice.

"Now if we died with Christ, we believe that we will also live with Him" (Romans 6:8).

You may not "feel" like you are dead to sin and alive to God, but don't trust your emotions. Trust the truth of God's Word. If you know Christ, you are now free to live and to choose; you are free to love Him with all your heart. This requires all of us to grow up because we are responsible for our choices.

The great theologian, Uncle Ben from *Spiderman,* told Peter Parker, "With great power comes great responsibility." That has a real spiritual ring to it. Living in the empowering reality of the exchange carries us into greater responsibility.

Responsible grown-ups make a choice of what to believe. You and I must choose whether to believe the absolute faithfulness of God or our emotions. If you have been adopted by God, if you have exchanged life with Jesus, then your life now belongs to Him. So choose to live by His strength and power, your human flesh is powerless over sin.

Whatever hang-ups, pains, fears, anxieties, guilt, or secret sins you have may be dropped off at the trash bin. *Now.* You have been crucified with Christ. You're not a little kid anymore; start exercising and walking out your grown-up faith in Him. *Consider* any bitterness, sin, anxieties, or anything else which haunts you as dead.

Session 1 **The Exchange**

Whatever sin you carry around with you (and think you will never overcome) has been defeated by the finished work of Christ on the cross.

All you have to do is choose. I urge you to make a choice consistent with *who you are*.

IDENTITY

I have always found it difficult to accept love from others; because of my insecurity I even fell into that pattern of subconsciously trying to sabotage relationships in order to test the love of friends and family.

This same insecurity also tainted my relationship with God. As a Christian, I often doubted the security of my salvation. I was obsessed with wondering if I was going to heaven. You probably know those insecurities: *"Since I still sin and am so spiritually weak, how can I know that I am truly His child?"* My question was born from my insecurity. Because I was rejected by my earthly father, I subconsciously worried that God would do the same thing. That was before I realized that not only would God never reject me, but He wanted me absolutely secure in who He had made me to be in Christ.

Personal identity is one of the primary issues of life. Knowing who we are, tracing the trail of our ancestry, and grasping our purpose in life are all components of personal identity. Some people go through life without ever being certain who they are.

I think a lack of identity is related to alienation from God.

Since He is our Eternal Father, all the trails lead to Him. So if our relationship to Him is broken or damaged, our identity is too. Before we were ever conceived in our mother's womb, God was our father. He predates our parents. If we can begin to grasp that, then we can move closer to being sure of who we are.

If we have been adopted by God through Christ, we are now firmly *secure* in Him. We are one of the "new creations" of whom Paul spoke in II Corinthians 5:17. The new creation that God has made you to be is holy and righteous because His holiness and righteousness is in our genes. He is, after all, our Father. According to Hebrews 10:10, **"We have been made holy through the sacrifice of the body of Jesus Christ once for all."**

As His child, our old lineage of sin and futility has been severed. When the Bible refers to our state of holiness in Christ, it is not playing some weird game with our head. It is not projecting some bizarre pretense that we are holy when we are not. The blood of Christ literally made us holy. There is nothing bizarre or tentative about

"Therefore if anyone is in Christ, there is a new creation; old things have passed away, and look, new things have come."
— 2 Corinthians 5:17

that. It's all in Him, not us. Yes, you can still stumble into sin, but to do so now goes against your very nature.

I have always loved the Dallas Cowboys. And, one of my all-time favorite players is Emmitt Smith. How could you not love Emmitt? Here was a guy too little to be a running back in professional football, yet he became the all-time rushing leader in the history of the NFL.

Few players have ever been as identified with a team as Emmitt Smith was with the Dallas Cowboys. So it was a disappointment to Cowboy fans when he played his last year in the NFL with the Arizona Cardinals. But when Emmitt retired from professional football, he did so as a Dallas Cowboy. In the Pro Football Hall of Fame, he will be enshrined as a Dallas Cowboy. Why? Because Emmitt Smith is a Dallas Cowboy through and through. For him to be known as anything else just doesn't ring true.

It is the same for you and me as God's children. Now that we have been united in Christ, we are to be forever identified with Him. For us to live any life other than the life of total dependence upon Jesus, is to live a lie and go against our very spiritual nature . . . and our identity.

"Because we know that Christ, having been raised from the dead, no longer dies. Death no longer rules over Him. For in that He died, He died to sin once for all; but in that He lives, He lives to God" (Romans 6:9-10).

THE KNOCKOUT

On the cross, Jesus gave sin, death, and Satan an eternal knockout blow. F.F. Bruce said that on the cross Jesus won a victory "that needs no second fight, and leaves no second foe".[4] That means that we can stop trying to get more forgiveness for our sins. We are now free. It also means that Jesus does not require our human effort to help Him live our Christian lives (Acts 17:25). He is not meant to be our copilot or even our pilot; He is our plane. We have to just climb on board, be seated, buckle our seat belts, and trust Him and what He says day by day, moment by moment. Just as Christ "lives to God," so do we.

His knockout also means that we are forever secure in Him. We don't have to worry about the power of sin, death, or Satan. We are not going to hell or slipping out of the Lord's grip. Why? Because "death no longer has mastery" over us. We are in Christ. For us to go to hell would mean that Christ would have to go with us (since we are now united with Him). Trust me—that is not going to happen.

We can rest in the absolute "foreverness" of what Jesus did for us. Our new familial and righteous identity in Him is neither tentative nor fragile. He paid for our sins with His holy blood. We can choose to believe now and live in that truth for the rest of our days, or we can just file it away as good "Christian information" and keep living in despair and defeat. Remember, we have the power to choose.

> Do you believe you are holy right now?

> What is the difference in accepting your holiness and trying to become holy?

EMOTIONS CAN LIE

Eugene Peterson wrote, "My feelings . . . tell me next to nothing about God or my relation to God. My security comes from who God is, not from how I feel. Discipleship is a decision to live by what I know about God, not by what I feel about him or myself or my neighbors. 'As the mountains are round about Jerusalem, so the Lord is round about his people.' The image that announces his dependable, unchanging, safe, secure existence of God's people comes from geology, not psychology."[5]

Think about it: our security has nothing whatsoever to do with how we feel. Peterson says that just as the mountains are not going away, so the Lord's surrounding of His people is not going to change. Ever. If you lived in Denver, you wouldn't wake up every morning wondering if the mountains were still standing. You would be certifiably insane if you first had to "feel in your heart" that the mountains were still there before being convinced they were there. So just as surely as the mountains remain around Jerusalem, so remains the faithfulness and love of God.

You don't have to think about it anymore. It's settled. You can stop doubting God and begin to rely on the immovable bedrock certainty of His Word. Christ has won the fight over your eternity; the only battle still raging is the one going in your head.

> Is God's opinion of you different than how you feel about yourself? How?

LIVING UP

Many of our problems are altitude issues. We live at such a low level that we are choking on the fumes of "this present age." Naturally, the atmosphere at the lower levels tends to be hazy and poisonous. That's why it's always healthy to press on up "the mountain" into the cleaner, clearer air of God's Presence.

Sometimes when we read the Bible from a lowland perspective, the message comes across as a severe, chastising, dismal list of rules. But what we are actually seeing is an invitation from Jesus (delivered through His servant Paul) to come up higher:

"So, you too consider yourselves dead to sin, but alive to God in Christ Jesus. Therefore do not let sin reign in your mortal body, so that you obey its desires. And do not offer any parts of it to sin as weapons for unrighteousness. But as those who are alive from the dead, offer yourselves to God, and all the parts of yourselves to God as weapons for righteousness. For sin will not rule over you, because you are not under law but under grace" (Romans 6:11-14).

Just imagine the Lord speaking to (with a smile), "Here's good news: You don't have to live down in that smoky, congested, biohazard of sin, evil desires, rules, and death. I personally invite you to come up to righteousness, grace, and full-color, full-throttle life."

Now there may be some skeptics out there (like me) who ask, "OK, Bible-boy, if I have moved up to the higher ground of a new nature and am truly united there with Christ and am holy in the sight of God, then why do I still sin?" That is a great question. Here is the answer: Because we choose to do so. We choose to remain in the lowland rather than moving up higher.

Victory of sin and eternal joy can be experienced *right now* if we choose to believe His Word and obey it. We don't have to live in the swamps of sin and that "try-and-fail" pattern of hopelessness. We have the power to choose to pitch our tent on higher ground. Victory is our choice.

Listen, the higher ground allows us to live as though we are literally dead to sin . . . because that is really what we are. The word "count" in verse 11 means "consider, reckon, to determine" or "to take into account." This word deals with the reality of your position. If you are dead to sin (that toxic lowland) but alive to God, then you live up high in communion and friendship with Him.

THE CULTURE OF THE HIGH GROUND

The high ground is a place of **"righteousness, peace, and joy in the Holy Spirit" (Romans 14:17).** That is a place above sin and justifying our sinful patterns of behavior. For example, I have a temper. My Mom and her father both had tempers. My cat has a temper. But I have no right to excuse my temper saying, "That's just the way I am." Why? Because I live in the higher ground of righteousness, peace, and joy. That is the culture which prevails there. No temper allowed. God has invited me to die to that temper and consider myself alive to Him who is **"slow to anger and full of faithful love" (Psalm 103:8).**

Like anyone who moves to a new country, sometimes we can lapse back into the customs and culture of our former homeland. If we keep resorting to old ways, customs, and traditions, then God, in His infinite wisdom and kindness, will sometime allow hardship to come into our lives. He loves us so much that He wants to bring us to the end of our selfishness (which is another way of describing the culture of our old residence). He allows pain to come into our little "Lord of the Ring" world to show us how much we need His higher life working in us. It's His way of reminding us of the new culture in which we live.

The culture of the higher ground assumes that we are victors, not victims. Victors make choices. Victims cannot. Victors have faith in God's promises. Victims do not.

Living in the high ground does not, however, mean that we live among temptation. But Paul says ". . . do not let sin reign." He didn't say "try your hardest to not sin." You see, Paul knew that, by the terms of the exchange, we have a choice of what to do about temptation. He said in verse 13 "don't sin but instead yield over your life to God" (Joel Engle paraphrase). We should not focus on "not sinning." Rather, our focus should be on our communion with God and our submission to Christ who now lives in us.

Here's the bottom line: We all experience temptation, but temptation should drive us to God before it drives us to sin. As citizens of the higher ground, we do have that choice. When sin lurks at our door, we have to turn to God with that temptation. We don't have to open the door.

> What are some practical ways you can incorporate the "new culture" into your daily life?
>
> Do you see Jesus' call to holiness as an invitation or an indictment?

☑ Take Away

☐ Read the first five chapters of Romans to deepen your understanding of the context of this study.
☐ Spend some time considering how this different look at salvation can influence your relationship with Jesus. Journal your thoughts.
☐ Commit Romans 6:4 to memory.

"Therefore we were buried with Him by baptism into death, in order that, just as Christ was raised from the dead by the glory of the Father, so we too may walk in a new way of life."
— Romans 6:4

Prayer

OH GOD, seeing as there is in Christ Jesus
An infinite fullness of all that we can want or desire,
May we all receive from him, grace upon grace;
Grace to pardon our sins, and subdue our iniquities;
To justify our persons and to sanctify our souls;
And to complete that holy change, that renewal of our hearts,
Which will enable us to be transformed
Into the blessed image in which you created us.
O make us all acceptable to be partakers
Of the inheritance of your saints in light.
Amen.

JOHN WESLEY

You'll find prayers written by
Christ-followers from way back at
the end of each session. Soak up
their wisdom and honesty as you
spend time alone with God.

Notes

_____
_____
_____
_____
_____
_____
_____
_____
_____
_____
_____
_____
_____
_____
_____
_____
_____
_____
_____
_____
_____
_____
_____
_____
_____
_____
_____
_____
_____
_____
_____
_____
_____
_____

SESSION 2

Exchanging Slavery

GOD CREATED our emotions as integral parts of our humanity. In His design, those emotions were to always be subject to the higher rule of God's will. The fall of man in Genesis 3 affected every part of humanity, including our emotional state.

The result is that human emotions no longer conform to the will of God; in fact, most of the time, emotions lead us away from the truth. Because many people, including Christians, continue to rely exclusively on emotions, sin is not treated as the evil it really is.

I travel pretty extensively within the Christian subculture. One of the most tragic developments of recent years is the absolute accommodation of sin in and by Christians. I continually meet believers who laugh about getting drunk, consistently speak in obscenity and profanity, live together before marriage, and accumulate so much debt that they cannot be free to give to the Lord.

While I am happy to see a larger understanding of grace, I am concerned that some are misapplying or even perverting the meaning of grace. True grace—that is, properly understood and fully embraced grace—does not result in an increase in sin but an increase in holiness.

EXCHANGING SLAVERY

ROMANS 6:15-23

LET'S TALK ABOUT SIN

I think many people (including Christians) think sin is God's personal kill-joy list. They imagine Him sitting in a blue funk, devising a list of don'ts which will keep everyone from having a good time.

In reality, sin is the devil's toxic prescription for destroying life.

"Sin will take you further than you wanted to go, keep you longer than you wanted to stay, and cost you more than you wanted to pay." I do not know who first said that, but it is one of the best descriptions of sin I've ever heard. Anyone considering a sexual affair, drugs, going into debt, or any other indulgence should stop and think about the deceptive and seductive nature of sin.

Sin is an ugly, tyrannical, and brutal slave master. It will never reveal the true destination, duration, or expense. Lives are ruined every day because people fail to understand the gravity of their choices.

Many law enforcement agencies use the web site Rate Your Risk *(rateyourrisk.org).* The site is an interactive test to evaluate personal vulnerability to various kinds of crime—murder, rape, robbery, burglary, etc. By asking lifestyle questions, it helps individuals evaluate their risk.

Many of the questions relate to what kind of car you drive, how much cash you carry, and the hours you work. However, a surprisingly large number of questions ask very pointed questions about moral character. These are actual questions from the survey:

1. How many acts of adultery have you committed (in the last two years)?

2. You are unmarried and you have dated a married person in the last year. How many dates with this married person?

3. You are unmarried and you steadily cohabit with one person but you have dated on the sly in the last year. Indicate your total the number of partners.

Now, understand that these questions are not being asked by "right-wing Christian nuts," or "Christian fundamentalists." These are being asked by behavioral scientists who have documented a link between "sin". and risk of being murdered, raped, shot, beaten, or burglarized.

That is an excellent modern-day, secular, interpretation of what Paul calls the wages of sin in Romans 6:23.

THE EXCHANGE—FREEDOM

"What then? Shall we sin because we are not under law but under grace? Absolutely not! Do you not know that if you offer yourselves to someone as obedient slaves, you are slaves of that one you obey—either of sin leading to death or of obedience leading to righteousness?" (Romans 6:15-16).

God's plan for us is *not* a peace treaty between His life and ours. We have to die to ourselves so that *His life* can flow into ours. He died to provide it. We must die to receive it, and through the cross, we have. Just like Jesus, we did not stay dead; we have been resurrected into a new life that is free from sin and alive to God. God has not called us to strive and strain with all of our might to conquer sin and then somehow, because of our effort, rise to the higher ground of life in Christ.

Neither does He leave us to just wander through life aimlessly trampling on His grace. We are now united with Christ.

Slavery is, of course, a diabolical and heartbreaking blight upon history. As such, it is also one of the best and most graphic pictures of Satan's design for life. Satan is a slave master. God's exchange of life is our underground railroad of freedom from the tyranny and brutality of Satan's design.

When Paul wrote Romans 6:15, it could sound like he was just repeating his original question from verse one. Even though some commentators believe that, I do not. The difference between verse one—"are we to continue in sin"—and verse 15—"shall we sin?"—is in the verb tense used in the original language (Greek).

In Romans 6:1, Paul is basically saying, "Should we keep on sinning now that Christ has defeated sin by the cross?" The phrase translated as "continue" or "keep on" is the Greek word *meno*. It refers to a house guest. Paul is saying that sin is no longer a welcome resident in our lives.[6]

I believe Ray Stedman captured the meaning of verse 15 when he wrote, "The other question is not, 'Shall we continue to abide in sin,' but, rather, 'Should we sin even once now that we are not under law but under grace?' That is the meaning of the question

Listen to the audio file "Depending on God in an Independent Society" while you read this session. Consider starting a similar discussion among your friends this week.

in Romans 6:15. Once we begin to realize the mighty power of Christ living in us, as opposed to the futility of trying to be good, we begin to experience some wonderful, great victories in our lives."[7]

In other words, whereas the Mosaic law dealt primarily with the external behavioral issues (don't murder, don't lie, etc.), the higher ground of living in the Spirit means that each detail of our life is free from the tyranny of sin. We don't have to tolerate or make peace with even one transgression. The power of the exchange gives us the freedom to live above the brutal slavery of sin in every area of life. That is freedom!

Consider this: Because of the exchange, Christians experience conviction of God's Holy Spirit within them when they sin. The law never produced that.

The Bible never claims that walking with God results in a life of ease or passivity. On the contrary, a healthy relationship with Jesus requires a living, active, daily-exercised faith because God's way of living is contradictory to our culture. Sometimes the battles of temptation are difficult and even painful. The Scriptures make it clear: The Christian life is difficult, demanding, and disciplined. We have no right to sin. God doesn't just shrug at even occasional lapses into sin. Thankfully, our God empowers (and expects) us to walk in total freedom by depending upon the life of Jesus Christ within us. Even with that victory, it is often difficult to deny ourselves and turn to the higher ground of Christ's rule. It takes practice.

I am a golfer. Golf is a tough game that takes an amazing amount of coordination and patience to be good at. For that reason, it is best to take lessons. When my golf instructor, Troy, first tried to fix my swing, his techniques "felt" terribly unnatural to me. Quickly sensing that my feelings had come into play, he reassured me that what he was doing was helping build a more *natural* swing. Well, it certainly didn't feel natural. However, as I began to internalize Troy's teaching, I started hitting the ball much better. After those first moments of awkward feelings, I experienced more joy and less frustration in my game.

Likewise, by embracing the difficulties of the Christian life and approaching those challenges with appropriate discipline, we move from frustration to joy. The further we move away from sin, the more we enjoy the game.

Now, go live victoriously … as a slave.

How do you practice letting Christ live through you?

How is God's definition of freedom different than our culture's?

Session 2 **The Exchange**

A NEW MEANING

Let's face it. Slavery is a bad word. In modern usage, it never has a good interpretation. In the New Testament, however, the word has a more complex meaning.

"But thank God that, although you used to be slaves of sin, you obeyed from the heart that pattern of teaching you were entrusted to, and having been liberated from sin, you became enslaved to righteousness" (Romans 6:17-18).

The word translated *slave* here is the Greek word *doulos*. To begin to understand what that word means, consider what Greek scholar, Kenneth Wuest, says about it: "...*doulos* means, 'one whose will is swallowed up in the will of another.' Paul argues that before salvation, the person's will was swallowed up in the will of Satan, but since he has been saved, his will is swallowed up in the sweet will of God."[8]

There you have it. We are all swallowed up by the will of another. As strange, even contorted, as it might sound, *we are created to be slaves*. The question is not whether we will be slaves, but exactly what we will be enslaved to. In our modern culture, we think that freedom means to live any way that we want. No constrictions at all. No authority at all. But living like that can never lead to freedom.

THE SEVERED BRANCH

True freedom is not doing whatever you desire to do; it is found in doing what you were meant to do. Let's go back to our apple tree (pages 8-11). The branch is only free as long as it remains attached to the seamless creation of the tree—roots flowing from the earth into the trunk, which courses to the limbs, which branch on out to bear flavorful fruit. When the branch is cut or torn from the tree and falls to the ground, it dies. Soon, the branch becomes dry and brittle; all life is gone.

It is precisely the same in our relationship to Christ. Jesus said, **"I am the vine, you are the branches; he who abides in Me, and I in him, he bears much fruit; for apart from Me you can do nothing" (John 15: 5)**. Only when we live in unbroken fellowship with Christ are we really free. When we go off on our own, we shrivel up and experience the emptiness of death. As Wuest suggests, we can be enslaved to Christ or to Satan.

So would you describe your life right now as being swallowed up in the sweet will of God? Having been rescued from slavery to Satan, that is what our lives should reflect.

We were under the harsh enslavement of Satan who hated us and drove us toward destruction. Now we are under the kind and generous rule of our Father who makes it possible for us to be satisfied in Him and Him alone. Doesn't it seem ridiculous for any believer to run back into their former life of slavery resulting in death after coming to an understand the great freedom enjoyed in slavery to Christ?

SLAVERY TO CHRIST

William Borden was born in 1887 into the Borden dairy dynasty. He lived a life of privilege and wealth. Borden yielded his life to Christ at an early age. After his education at Yale and Princeton, he could have easily taken over his family's fortune and lived a life of comfort and ease. But Bill Borden knew something of great wisdom and value: *he was a slave to Christ*. He did not belong to himself.

Many were shocked when he walked away from all his wealth in exchange for living out his life as a missionary. Many more thought it was tragic when Borden died of spinal meningitis in Egypt trying to reach Muslims with the gospel. He was only 25 years old. Was his life a waste?

Some might say so. They would argue that Borden had the opportunity to do so much more with his life, experience so many more things, and exercise so much more freedom than he did when he chose to bind himself to Christ. That argument is flawed, however, because it assumes that freedom is the same thing as living to please yourself; it's failing to understand that living a life apart from God is really slavery to sin.

That type of slavery is a vicious cycle that has no end apart from Christ. The more you try to feed your emptiness with the things the world offers, the more miserable you can become. You wonder how this "freedom" could be such a downer.

A slave has no will but the will of his master. To serve Christ means to have no will but His. That's easier said than done in our rights-focused society. In reality, we have no rights. We have died and are now united with Christ. He is our life. We serve Him. And that is where we can find true freedom and satisfaction.

How do you define satisfaction?

How have you experienced freedom in serving?

JESUS' VIEW OF FREEDOM AND SERVICE

Celebrity culture has imposed a warped perspective on the way we define significance. That same attitude has warped the Christian mind and the church. We celebrate famous Christian athletes, recording artists, movie stars, and politicians.

How did Jesus see His role? **"The Son of Man did not come to be served, but to serve, and to give His life—a ransom for many" (Mark 10:45).**

Paul wrote that **". . . even Christ did not please Himself" (Romans 15:3).** Think about that. As Lord of the world, Jesus could have arranged His life for comfort. Instead, He rejected selfishness and pride. He humbled Himself to become a servant. He could have made the whole world bow down and worship Him. Yet He gave up His will to do the will of His Father. So what kind of life does that kind of submission bring us?

If you become swallowed up in the will of God, you must face the reality that you will not have an easy, carefree life. As He did with William Borden, God may lead you into a life of sacrificial service. He certainly led His Son down that road. The same kind of fate awaited the writer of Romans.

Paul started most of his letters by identifying himself to his readers. Incredibly, for a man with such an impressive resume, he sometimes introduced himself as a servant or prisoner of Christ. Paul's slavery to Christ cost him much. He suffered in so many ways. The lives of Jesus, Paul, and William Borden might make us ask: *"Why anyone would want to be swallowed up in the will of God?"*

I find Paul's words to the Philippian church a very moving response to that question: **". . . whatever was to my profit I now consider loss for the sake of Christ. What is more, I consider everything a loss compared to the surpassing greatness of knowing Christ Jesus my Lord, for whose sake I have lost all things. I consider them rubbish, that I may gain Christ . . . " (Philippians 3:7-8).** Paul counted his life as nothing compared to the higher ground of just knowing Christ. The same can be true for you. You may suffer, but think of the sweet communion with Him that can only be found in great service… and sacrifice.

Does your slavery to Christ lead you to count this world as rubbish for the sake of Christ? Does it make you want to serve Christ with all of my heart and soul?

The Bible reminds us that **"No one can be a slave of two masters, since either he will hate one and love the other, or be devoted to one and despise the other. You cannot be slaves of God and of money" (Matthew 6:24).**

Thank God that He has exchanged our old nature with His Spirit. We have cashed in slavery to that lower realm of death and destruction for the higher slavery under the magnificent and generous Master of all creation.

> Do you like the idea of being God's slave?

> What is most concerning to you about characterizing your Christian experience as one of slavery?

FORGETTING OBEDIENCE

The older you get, the more you forget. Remember that.

I forget where I laid the keys to my car all the time. I spend hours a week looking for them. We forget the things we promise. We forget who won the Super Bowl three years ago. Major news headlines quickly become yesterday's news. But I also think we have very selective memories. We remember the things we want to remember (like our own birthdays) and forget the things we don't want to remember (like our high school pictures).

We want our way and our rights so badly that we forget that God is God. When that happens, we start to take matters into our own hands. Usually, we get ourselves into big trouble and quickly realize the mistakes we have just made. We become unhappy in our jobs and relationships. The lack of satisfaction usually makes us realize that we are nothing without His life working in us.

If we are wise, we run back to Him. We run back to obedience.

As you know by now, Jesus Christ has set us free from the bondage of sin. It no longer has mastery over us because we were united with Him in His death, burial, and resurrection. Our old life of sin was killed and buried. The life it produced has been completely replaced by a new life in Christ. This is not a theory; it is a reality for your life right now.

Because of that reality, the love, power, and joy of the Lord move in your life just as the life of the apple tree moves from the roots on out to the tips of its branches. However, many fail to experience the surging power of His presence on a continual basis. How can we realize the love, power, and joy of the Lord in greater measure in our everyday life?

Great question. The answer: *obedience*.

THE ROLE OF GRATITUDE

God has done so much for us. The way we live our lives should exemplify our thankfulness. There is a strong link between our sense of gratitude and our level of obedience.

People who are grateful tend to joyfully obey those who lead them. A relationship of righteous love will almost always produce obedience as a feature of the relationship. Children who love and are grateful for their parents joyfully obey them. Employees who appreciate their company and their bosses are able to obey company and management directives with joy and a clear conscience. Members of healthy churches almost always turn their gratitude into fruitful and happy obedience of the church leadership.

On the other hand, I believe that most of our disobedience begins with a thankless heart. We lose our contentment with God. When we lose our sense of appreciation, we also lose the desire to obey. That is true of children toward parents, citizens toward law enforcement, and Christians toward church leaders. Once that gratitude is lost, it is human nature to seek satisfaction in pleasure, money, entertainment, and other diversions. The relationship between gratitude and obedience is clearly seen throughout our culture.

Obviously, we live in an age that despises and rejects authority. Movie stars, singers, athletes, and authors "rage against the machine" of the establishment. No one wants to obey any form of authority. Is it just a coincidence that we live in an age of both arrogance and ingratitude?

OBEDIENCE CONFIRMS THE EXCHANGE

In obedience to God, we confirm the exchange of His superior life for our sinful one. Every act of obedience expresses that we have rejected our own way and received His higher and perfect will for our life.

The exchanged life is about God infusing His life into yours as you submit to Him. We don't become robots. Rather, through the exchange, we become all that we were created to be.

Sometimes, however, we are just disobedient. We don't trust God, or we don't like what His Word reveals about ourselves, and we take off running. It reminds me of the story of Jonah and the great fish. Jonah didn't want to obey God, and he wound up in a most undesirable situation. How many times has that happened to you and me? God is trustworthy. He has done more than enough to earn our trust. He has set us free from sin. He has adopted us into His family. By immersing ourselves in the truth of His everlasting love, we can be truly motivated to live life His way and not ours.

Listen to the Apostle Paul's prayer for you and me: **"I pray that you, being rooted and firmly established in love, may be able to comprehend with all the saints what is the length and width, height and depth of God's love . . ." (Ephesians 3:17b-18).**

God's authority doesn't oppress us. It liberates us from the power of sin, which is death. He is a loving Father who always has our best interests at heart.

As the father of two beautiful daughters, there is nothing I wouldn't do to guarantee their happiness. I would easily lay my life down to protect them at all costs. My wife and daughters are the greatest treasures I have besides Christ. Yes, I discipline my girls when they disobey. I don't do it because I love to see them cry. I do it because I don't want to see them die. I want them to stop running towards the street when I tell them to stop. When their little hands raise to touch the hot stove, I want them to obey me when I tell them to back away. When they grow older, I want them to have authentic character and to love God. I want them to know the difference between right and wrong. I desperately desire for them to experience the joy of freedom under my authority. That is exactly how God feels about you, except God loves you perfectly. My love for my daughters is an imperfect love. God's love for you is unequaled. God wants you to enjoy life under His authority because you absolutely trust where He is lovingly leading you. Think about the words to this old hymn:

> Trust and obey
> For there's no other way
> To be happy in Jesus
> But to trust and obey

What role does faith play in obedience?

Are there circumstances in your life that seem to contradict the love of God?

BELIEVE. RECEIVE. BECOME.

When I played basketball in high school, our coach made us practice free throws over and over again. We ran sprints until we could barely breathe. I remember ball handling drills day after day after day. We went over our offensive strategies relentlessly. As much as we hated practice, the coach never let up. Slowly, the repetition became second-nature to us. Do you suppose our coach knew that would happen?

Session 2 **The Exchange**

When it came time for us to play our first game, all of the practice, drills, and repetition converged, and we were mean sports machines. In the same way, in Romans 6: 19-21, Paul is drilling us about the idea that our old nature died and that we now have a new nature in Christ. Like any good coach, he is beating it into our very being *so that it will become a way of life for us*. It is one thing to say that you believe your sins are forgiven and that you now have the power through Christ to overcome sin. It is another thing to live it out daily.

There is a life-changing pattern here for us: *Believe. Receive. Become.*

First, *we believe* the truth about The Exchange. Second, we *receive* the impartation—the osmosis—of it. The result of that process is that we *become* conformed to His image (Romans 8:29).

Jesus related this truth to His disciples. They struggled to believe what He said. Over and over again, we hear Jesus urging His young followers towards *belief*. Finally they heard the word, but they didn't fully *receive* it. Therefore, much of their early experiences were in failure and frustration. You can't *become* who Christ wants you to be until you *believe* and *receive*.

CHRISTIANITY 101

Sadly, too much of the contemporary church ignores this progression to maturity. Instead, Christian culture has imposed a modern Greek model of intellectualizing belief. As a result, too many Christians walk in a superficial understanding of Christianity rather than a deep personal relationship with Jesus. I am concerned that we are trading the organic for the organization. It seems that we are so focused on behavior that we are very willing to trade rules for relationship. But institutions can never replace intimacy.

The mechanical functions of Bible study, prayer, fasting, church attendance, and other disciplines are important, to the process. However, the purpose of those disciplines is *that we become conformed to His image*. That doesn't happen through programs, campaigns, or marketing schemes.

Francis Schaeffer once said, "There is no mechanical solution to true spirituality or the true Christian life. Anything that carries the mark of the mechanical upon it is a mistake. It is not possible to say, 'Read so many of the chapters of the Bible every day, and you will have this much sanctification.' . . . This is purely a mechanical solution, and it denies the whole reality of Christian position."[9]

"I am using a human analogy because of the weakness of your flesh. For just as you offered the parts of yourselves as slaves to moral impurity, and to greater and greater lawlessness, so now offer them as slaves to righteousness, which results in sanctification. For when you were slaves of sin, you were free from allegiance to righteousness. And what fruit was produced then from the things you are now ashamed of? For the end of those things is death" (Romans 6:19-21).

I love the way Paul speaks so plainly; he has a way of crashing truth right through our thick skulls. Here he reminds us that sin was once second nature to us (when we presented our bodies as slaves to impurity and lawlessness). We did not have or need memory verses on how to sin; it was natural.

The discipline of the exchanged life is what I like to call the discipline of dependence. We are training ourselves to rely on the power of Christ each day so we can see His life radiating through ours. So just as a coach turns goofball kids into a disciplined, soaring basketball team, so Christ can turn us into spiritually mature, Christ-as-second-nature Christians.

What we are studying here is the very basic, fundamental truth of Christianity, but I believe that this teaching has been greatly overlooked by the mainstream church. Most teaching on the Christian life is about doing things for God. God has a method for the way His children are to live. That method is depending upon the person of Jesus Christ to live His life through our unique personalities.

Don't get me wrong here. I am not saying that spiritual disciplines like Bible study, worship, or other disciplines are bad. Those things are wonderful and extremely important *but only in their proper order.* They must never become mechanical or replace the lifestyle of communion and dependence upon God.

What is the current purpose of spiritual disciplines in your life?

How do you think God wants you to view those disciplines?

THE BENEFIT

When I was 18, I had the metabolism of a hummingbird. No matter how much I ate, I never gained weight. Now if I even think about a peanut butter and jelly sandwich, it seems like I instantly gain two pounds.

When I diet, I need to see results pretty quickly, or I get discouraged. I need to see some benefits of all my hard work in order to keep going. At this point in our study, you may be asking, "What is the real benefit of knowing all this stuff about the Christian life?"

Jesus came to earth to bring us life. Real life. Abundant life. Eternal life. Jesus came to rescue His people from the bondage of sin and cause His life to flow into and through them. Now, our existence on earth has purpose. That purpose is to love Christ and focus our lives on Him. Embracing these truths from Romans can move us into the life God has always intended for us to live.

WHAT IS "ETERNAL LIFE?"

"But now, since you have been liberated from sin and become enslaved to God, you have your fruit, which results in sanctification—and the end is eternal life! For the wages of sin is death, but the gift of God is eternal life in Christ Jesus our Lord" (Romans 6:22-23).

What does Paul mean when he uses the phrase "eternal life?" Do you think he's referring to reclining on soft, cotton clouds? Is he talking about heaven? Or is there something else in this phrase that we are missing?

Paul wasn't just talking about the hereafter when he mentioned eternal life. Eternal life is a quality and a dimension of life, not a time off somewhere "in the sweet bye and bye." It includes heaven when we die, but, the idea is larger than that. Eternal life is God's life. As such, it is the essence of life which He gives to us. Eternal life begins *now* with Christ. The benefit of dying to self and allowing Christ to live His life through ours is that we can receive this eternal kind of life. All the joy, peace, and love you could ever need—or want—is found in Christ and Christ alone.

That eternal kind of life gets worked out in various ways during our life on earth.

HEALING FOR BROKEN LIVES

Many Christians live in bondage when they don't have to. Because they don't know that they are forgiven completely, they run from God when they sin instead of running to Him. They are simply not secure in their relationship with God.

Much of the brokenness which surrounds us is due to the rampant and pervasive social breakdown of our times. In this day of divorce and the collapse of the family unit, millions of people have deep emotional wounds that cause serious damage.

Christians are certainly not exempt from the fallout of sin in our generation. You may have grown up in a broken family like I did. If so, you probably still sometimes wonder if you are really loved by anybody.

This is why it is so important to understand our new identity in Christ. We are no longer slaves to the wounds of the past. That doesn't mean we don't feel the pain, but it does mean we don't have to be destroyed by it. We have been set free from sin, from bitterness, from self-pity, and from hopelessness.

All of us "broken people," can made whole again through the exchange of life with Christ. To be in Christ means our lives are now intertwined with His wholeness. We are, therefore, whole and complete because He is whole and complete.

I will never forget walking into my junior-high cafeteria and seeing the "cool" people. I was not in with them. They did not recognize me as a whole person. Of course, I thought, "If only I could be in their group, life would be great." I so desperately wished one of them would walk across the room and invite me to be in their group. Psychologists would say that I was projecting; I believed that acceptance from them would make me a whole and complete person. Of course, that was an illusion. People never make us whole.

Before we knew Christ, we were incomplete people on the outside looking in. Then Christ stepped into our lives, and now we have an eternal connection with Him that can never be severed. This relationship "is nothing less than a vital, organic, intimate union with Jesus Christ, involving a shared life and love."[10] That shared life is more than sufficient to make us whole.

A FUTURE AND A HOPE

We live in hopeless times. Many kids today admit they don't expect to live beyond their teen years. Who can blame them? Global warming, the AIDS epidemic, threat of armed conflict, and natural disasters all seem to give a sense of hopelessness.

In the exchanged life, we can begin to see circumstances through the vision of Jesus. With His eyes, we can see past present circumstances to a clear vantage point of the God of Jeremiah. I bring up Jeremiah because the people of his day were in sore need of hope. The nation of Israel was ruthlessly conquered and sent into exile. Out of that void of despair came the ancient voice which still speaks to all who receive the life of Christ: **"For I know the plans I have for you . . . plans for your welfare, not for disaster, to give you a future and a hope" (Jeremiah 29:11).**

When we receive His life, an enormous hope and splendid future open up before us.

Session 2 **The Exchange**

PROSPERITY

Jesus told His disciples (and, by extension, us): **"Remain in me, and I in you. Just as a branch is unable to produce fruit by itself unless it remains on the vine, so neither can you unless you remain in me" (John 15:4)**.

One of the benefits of His exchange of life with us is that we become fruitful, or prosperous. The biblical view of prosperity is not the same as the one presented by our consumerist American economy. Today, when we hear the word *prosperity*, we think of flashy clothes, mansions on golf courses, Jaguars, and expensive jewelry.

But in the Bible, prosperity denotes peace and well-being. It is a state of great security and strength. When Christ's life pushes through the branches of His vine, it causes fruit to appear. That is prosperity. And in a biblical sense, prosperity has vast moral and ethnical dimensions.

I admit that we can all attain some degree of morality in our own strength. However, morality comes from behavioral modification. You can make yourself do good things, but that does not begin to measure up to the holiness which comes from God. The only way to prosper in holiness is to receive His life each and every day.

In short, eternal life is the highest quality of life in existence and as unimaginable as it may sound, it is yours. All you have to do is exchange your life for His.

Which of those benefits of external life most resonates with you?

How does your idea of quality of life differ from God's?

Take Away

☐ Check out a copy of *Uncle Tom's Cabin* from the local library to expand your picture of slavery.
☐ Engage in a conversation surrounding this question: "How do you measure your spirituality?"
☐ Commit Romans 6:14 to memory.

"For sin will not rule over you, because you are not under law but under grace." — Romans 6:14

Session 2 **Exchanging Slavery**

Prayer

OH GOD early in the morning I cry to you.
Help me to pray
And to concentrate my thoughts on you;
I cannot do this alone.

In me there is darkness,
But with you there is light;
I am lonely, but you do not leave me;
I am feeble in heart, but with you there is help;
I am restless, but with you there is peace.
In me there is bitterness, but with you there is patience;
I do not understand your ways,
But you know the way for me.

O heavenly Father,
I praise and thank you for the peace of the night;
I praise and thank you for this new day;
I praise and thank you for all your goodness
And faithfulness throughout my life.

You have granted me many blessings;
Now let me also accept what is hard from your hand.
You will lay on me no more than I can bear.
You make all things work together for good for your children.

DIETRICH BONHOEFFER

Notes

Notes

Session 2 **The Exchange**

Notes

SESSION 3

Exchanging the Law

I ATTENDED Stuart Hall Catholic School from kindergarten through fifthth grade. I was not a model student. I had a bad case of ADHD; unfortunately for me, the term ADHD did not exist in those days. Rather than being treated or counseled, I was simply dubbed "a troublemaker." I was in continual trouble for talking in class, fighting with other kids, and general misbehavior.

The school's worst punishment was the dreaded red chair. Located right outside Mr. Glaub's office, it was the place where the rowdy ones awaited their indictment, trial, and punishment. Because the chair was so visible, the whole school would pass and stare at the condemned trouble maker. Those like me, who could not obey the rules, were seen there often.

Many of us carry a "red chair" view of God and the Christian life. From the vantage point of the red chair, God is always looking at us with a frown; He could never be happy with us or anything we do. At any moment, His anger may explode, and when it does, it will not be pretty. I think we are driven to that kind of thinking because we are measuring our relationship with God by our ability to keep all the rules we find throughout the Bible, particularly in the Old Testament. If those rules—or laws—are the measuring stick of our spirituality, then we have a distorted idea of the purpose of the law.

Exchanging the Law

ROMANS 7:1-8

THEOLOGY FROM THE RED CHAIR

You probably never have sat in Mr. Glaub's red chair, but you probably know the feeling well. I think most Christians don't just sit in God's red chair; they live there.

Here is the good news: That fearful scenario is a myth. Red chair theology is a con job. God took care of the problem of sin by sending Jesus to take the ultimate punishment for us. Now God looks at us as truly holy—not because of our performance but because of what Christ has done on our behalf. He has freed us from the condemnation of living under the law.

So, what was/is the purpose of the law? I mean, if God always knew Jesus would free us from living under it, then why did the law exist in the first place?

"Since I am speaking to those who understand law, brothers, are you unaware that the law has authority over someone as long as he lives?" (Romans 7:1).

THE LAW: GOD'S SERVANT

God created the law as His servant. Its purpose is to bring us to the end of ourselves and lead us into communion with Him. It was never God's plan for humans to approach Him by trying really hard to obey the law—not in the Old Testament and not in the New Testament. Nobody has ever been saved from sin by obeying the law. God did not create the law to regenerate a sinful heart; the law cannot give you the desire to obey it. The human heart, apart from Christ, has no desire or ability to obey God.

The law serves God by revealing the depths of human need. Far from being a spiritual stepping stone, God's law is actually meant to terrify us from ever trying to attempt to reach God by good deeds. The law's job is to show us our incredible need for a Savior. The law is designed to lead us to Christ.

So in one sense, the law reveals the problem but doesn't give the solution. Jesus is, and always was, the solution. The law is a cold stone; it carries the etched inscription of perfection. Jesus is the living, warm, full-blooded fulfillment of perfection. Not only that, but He is also—through the exchange—our perfection!

All of the rituals of the nation of Israel—like the sacrifices and temple ordinances—were actually images of God's plan for redemption through the future coming of

Jesus Christ. As the author of Hebrews said, **"The law is only a shadow of the good things that are coming—not the realities themselves. For this reason the law can never, by the same sacrifices repeated endlessly year after year, make perfect those who draw near to worship"** (Hebrews 10:1).

Here is a simple truth: Regardless of when people lived in history, as long as their lives exist away from faith in Christ, they are under the condemnation of the Law: **"For all who rely on the works of the law are under a curse, because it is written: 'Cursed is everyone who does not continue doing everything written in the book of law'"** (Galatians 3:10). They are a prisoner to their sinful nature. Being "under the Law" means that a person is separated from Christ; they have not experienced the deliverance of the cross.

But, thank God, because of the exchange, we have now been set free from sin. We have a new nature that desires to obey God and to love Him with a whole heart. The law only serves God (and us) by revealing the great gap between God's perfection and our own ability to measure up.

Jesus closed the gap.

Listen to the audio file "Behavior Modification vs. Knowing God" as you study the purpose of the law. How is your perspective changing?

WHY IS THAT DIFFICULT TO GRASP?

Not too long ago I asked a friend how he was doing in his Christian life. His face clouded over as he stumbled and stammered. He was just so busy with his work and college schedules. He tried, really tried, to read the Bible and some good Christian books, but just couldn't stick with them because of his chaotic schedule.

Then, he just blurted out, "I feel like I can never do enough for God."

Do you feel that way?

I told him—and I tell you—that the cross of Christ killed our sinful nature. We have been made alive in Christ. We are new creations, totally loved by God. God wouldn't love my friend, or you, any more if he and you read the Bible cover to cover every day. Yet, for some reason, we insist on living under the curse of law, even knowing that Christ had set us free. That insistence on getting back under the law kills the joy and victory of our new relationship with God.

I hope you are beginning to grasp that the Christian life is a love relationship with Christ based on what He did for us at Calvary. It is not about trying not to sin. His work on the cross doesn't leave us in that "living any way we please" state either. God doesn't want us to measure our lives by our accomplishments or failures.

Our life can only be measured by Christ and His sacrifice. We are now invited into a life of obedience and fellowship with Him.

> What role does the law play in your relationship to God?

> How do you know if you're "doing good" in your spiritual life?

MYSTERY OF MARRIAGE

From an early age, many girls dream of their wedding day. Guys don't. Girls start planning the color scheme, the dresses, the music, and every small detail of their wedding day long before they have a fiance. Guys start thinking about it a week before the ceremony.

The Apostle Paul was a true guy. After all, he called marriage a "great mystery" (Ephesians 5:31–32). I can resonate with that. I still remember my sense of wonder when I saw my stunning bride Valerie walking down the aisle. But Paul saw the mystery in a different way. He knew that marriage is like a diamond; as you turn it in the light, it gathers radiant rays which stream out of heaven. As he gazed into the diamond, he saw truths far beyond the earthly institution of marriage.

In Romans 7:2-3, Paul spins the diamond of marriage to reveal how death dissolves the reach and authority of the law. Eugene Peterson interprets Paul's words like this:

"A wife is legally tied to her husband while he lives, but if he dies, she's free. If she lives with another man while her husband is living, she's obviously an adulteress. But if he dies, she is quite free to marry another man in good conscience, with no one's disapproval" (Romans 7:2-3, *The Message*).

Paul continues here with the very same thought of the previous verse—that the law only carries jurisdiction while a person lives. For example, Enron CEO Ken Lay was convicted on 10 counts of securities fraud and other charges related to the historic collapse of Enron. But, while he was awaiting sentencing, he suddenly died. Upon his death, the presiding judge abated his conviction.

Likewise Paul reminds us that through Christ's death, we also died. Therefore, the law—and whatever "convictions" it carries over us—is abated.

FREE TO REMARRY

When God gave Moses the 10 Commandments, man had an inscription in stone which outlined God's "moral order." Nothing wrong with that. It was a wonderful start. The law actually gave people a reasonable facsimile of what God wanted to see in individuals, families, communities, and nations.

But that moral order proved to be a difficult "husband;" he was not sensitive to the flesh and blood needs of his wife. He just stood in the home and gave her rules about marriage. He didn't help her; he was not caring and tender to his wife. He just knew the rules and regulations of what she was supposed to be. No romance at all. He was not Spirit.

Naturally, she wanted out of that cold and loveless marriage. Then her husband died.

The metaphorical woman here represents you and me under the law. The law was breaking our hearts because we could never measure up to its impossibly high standards. Because of our sinful nature, we could not escape the condemnation of our perfect husband. As people who were slaves to sin, we were just stuck in a very unhappy marriage. It may be hard for us to understand in our age of quick and easy divorce, but in God's plan, marriage is for life; the only way out is death.

John MacArthur explains this verse by saying, "Paul's point is simply this: A married person is bound by law to his or her spouse only as long as the spouse lives. If your spouse dies, you are no longer bound by law to him or her. You are not bound in marriage to a corpse for the rest of your life! The law of marriage binds people only while they are alive."[11]

Jesus Christ's death, burial, and resurrection destroyed the hopeless marriage that we lived under. The law, our eternally critical and condemning husband, is dead, and we are now free to marry someone else.

The woman in Paul's word picture is now re-married to Christ. Her second marriage has everything the first lacked: love, intimacy, and a husband committed to her joy and success in life. We as Christ-followers are the "woman" in this biblical metaphor.

As we enter further into the intimacy of our marriage to Jesus, we find that He helps us to become the very image of all that Father God ever envisioned for us. Because He is Spirit, He breathes life into every detail and nuance of life. And because of that, we are being changed.

> Why do you think the Bible uses marriage as a metaphor for our relationship to Jesus?

How do the marriages you have observed influence your understanding of that metaphor?

A LITTLE ROMANCE

I so enjoy my relationship with Valerie. I love her deeply. And besides that, I really like her. Every feature of this woman is beautiful. God did such a wonderful job in her. We love walking through life and marriage together. Our romance is wonderfully pleasant and thrilling.

The Christian life is about *enjoying* our relationship with Christ. Jesus is the Husband of the church (Ephesians 5:23, Revelation 21:2). As Spirit, He brings the romance to our faith walk in a way the previous husband, the law, never did or could.

The law was powerless to help us live righteous lives; it just told us when we didn't live up to what was "expected." The Law was "the standard," but it never helped us. The law didn't and couldn't hold us in its arms. It simply did not have the "husbandly" capacity to be able to impart any kind of joy, confidence, or enchantment to us.

Have you ever noticed how love transforms people? Not everyone in the world looks like a movie star. It's amazing to see the effect of love on those of us who do not look like Brad Pitt. Over time, regardless of physical appearance, something magical happens when someone is loved; they become gorgeous. Not much can rival the power of simply being loved.

The love of Christ does that to us. The old husband, law, could not bring that to us because love was not involved.

HIGHER THAN LAW

Don't get me wrong—the law is, in itself, not bad. The problem comes when we use the law as the basis of our relationship to God.

You see, God never saw the law as an end in itself. It reflected His perfection and symmetry. But God always knew that the law was only a billboard. The words in the law described and required something, but it couldn't actually come down from its lofty position and help us to fulfill it. God wasn't surprised that the law couldn't do that; He never intended for it to be so.

When people got hold of the law, they turned it into a means of "behavior modification." They missed the heart and soul of what God was trying to teach them about the coming Messiah. In the hands of people, law always becomes totalitarian (whether in civil or religious government). The real problem for us today is not the law, but legalism—that attempt by people and organizations to conform us to an earthy view of "perfection" or utopia.

But the Spirit breathes His life into us. And, over time, He radiantly imparts the surpassing transcendence of Christ's righteousness to us.

The exchanged life is not about working hard to fulfill the law, but about Christ loving us into a reflection of what the law intended. We are married to Him now. Our new relationship is secure, delightful, romantic, and absolutely transforming. Because of our union, we are free from the condemnation of the law, but also empowered to fulfill it as we walk in step with the Spirit of Christ.

That's good news—even great news—because we needed something much more drastic to happen to us than just behavior adjustment.

BEYOND BOTTLE-ROCKETS

Have you ever noticed how we try to find a bargaining position with God? We compare our "little sins" (always little in our eyes) with the bigger sins which we see so flagrantly around us.

Driving I-40 just east of Oklahoma City, I knew I that life was good and that I was within 5 miles per hour of the speed limit. Suddenly, a state trooper pull in behind me. Dry mouth. Sweaty palms. *Dear God, please* . . .

Rolling my window down, I politely explained to the 7-foot-tall, wide-shouldered, agent-of-God's-wrath that I was trying, really trying to go the speed limit. After gazing at my drivers license like it was pond scum, he sternly announced, "Mr. Engle, you were going 4 miles over the speed limit." My sinful mind thought, "you pulled me over for *that?* There are all of these terrible criminals running around and you pull me over for going 4 miles over the speed limit? Give me a break." He didn't. And he didn't have to. The law is the law, regardless of how big or little I perceived my infraction to be.

God doesn't assign categories and levels of sin. You see, the problem is *not* sin as action; the problem is our *sinful nature.* We think in perverse ways because that is our natural state. It is the "default mode" of our earth-formed minds. And our nature is what Jesus touches. He doesn't reform it; He replaces it with His own. The exchange is about His dying so that we could live. When we try to measure up to God in our human strength we fail and do so miserably. We are like a bottle-rocket trying to go for the moon. It's never going to happen.

You see, living in Christ is not about trying to "do better" or finding bargaining room with God. It is about walking in the "newness of life" that we have in Christ. On the cross, Christ paid for our sins and made us holy. He died so that we could live. That's the exchange.

"Therefore, my brothers, you also were put to death in relation to the law through the crucified body of the Messiah, so that you may belong to another— to Him who was raised from the dead—that we may bear fruit for God" (Romans 7:4).

When Jesus died, *all* who would ever trust Him died with Him. So, in effect, we were clinched—hidden—in His great hand when He died . . . and when He was resurrected.

As Paul explained to the Colossian Christians: **"For you died, and your life is hidden with the Messiah in God. When the Messiah, who is your life, is revealed, then you also will be revealed with Him in glory " (Colossians 3:3-4).**

WHAT TO DO WITH FORMER ENEMIES

The phrase "hidden in Christ" has always been meaningful to me. I like it because it speaks clearly about our position; it answers the question of where we are. Because of what Jesus has done at the cross, no matter where we are physically—school, work, home, gym, wherever—we are in Christ. That is particularly meaningful when you consider that formerly we were enemies of God. I don't know about you, but I wouldn't enjoy spending that kind of time with my enemies. Neither did Jesus, so He simply turned His enemies into His friends.

Our old identity as a sinner and His enemy was destroyed by the work of Christ on the cross. Now that we hidden in Christ, nothing can break the new bonds of our friendship with God.

As a result of that new friendship, your largest and perpetual identity is: Friend of God. You are not *primarily* a doctor, accountant, student, or housewife. You are not tall, short, small, or large. You are not rich, poor, cool, or uncool. You are one of God's friends. That surpasses every other identity and will never change.

In the movie, *The Bourne Identity*, Jason Bourne is a secret agent who suffers from amnesia. He can't remember his name, his job, his hometown, or anything else. Many Christians live like Jason Bourne. They don't know who they are in Christ. They have forgotten that Christ loves them, forgave them, and made them holy by His sacrifice on the cross. They go through their lives living in compromise, emptiness, guilt, and shame because of their spiritual amnesia. Tragically, they go on and on searching for fulfillment in life when Christ is all they will ever need.

As those who died through His death and have been raised from the dead into His resurrection life, we now have His eternal power living in us. Because of that eternal power, we can take this reality beyond "good theology" and put it into practice. We can live it out, joyfully and successfully.

What does the phrase "hidden in Christ" mean to you?

Does the law have any use in the exchanged life?

RELEASED!

"For when we were in the flesh, the sinful passions operated through the law in every part of us and bore fruit for death. But now we have been released from the law, since we have died to what held us, so that we may serve in the new way of the Spirit and not in the old letter of the law" (Romans 7:5-6).

In the World War II movie, *The Great Raid*, American prisoners faced certain execution by their captors in a Philippine concentration camp. This true story does not flinch in showing the brutality that the American soldiers suffered. Finally, in the crescendo of the movie, the Americans launch a risky and daring raid to set the prisoners free. The rescue is highly successful. Prisoners who thought they were going to die instead walk out of prison into freedom.

Can you imagine those soldiers rejoicing outside the gates of their prison for a few minutes and then choosing to go back into the POW camp for the remainder of their lives? Of course not. Yet many have been set free from the prison of sin and from the law by the work of Christ on the cross. But after a short time of rejoicing and dancing, they wander back into the prison dungeon.

We have been released from the prison of hate, lust, jealously, bitterness, shame, and drunkenness. We are free to live in love, joy and peace. We are free to run into a whole new way of life. Yet, we voluntarily return back into prison life. Why?

PRISON AS A WAY OF LIFE

Criminologists and prison officials know that many people return to prison because it represents a "safe" and structured environment. Prison gives some predictability to an otherwise chaotic world. Many that return have consciously or subconsciously decided that chains are better than the uncontrollable nature of "life on the outside."

I have often noticed that when people try to live life on their own terms, they often turn to what they view as "the law of the Bible" and become legalistic. Out of their inherent sense of guilt and shame, they return to the "safe and structured environment" of their well-worn lists of rules. They just cannot accept the wondrous beauty of release.

This way of life can be challenging and frightening. We may be a little uncomfortable with our new freedom, but Jesus is not. *He* isn't challenged or frightened by life beyond the prison walls. In fact, He is very comfortable and confident in life beyond the "safety" of legalism. That is where He wants to lead us, and perhaps that is where we would go if we were not so afraid of "life on the outside." But fear is a powerful motive.

I failed my driving test twice as a teenager. The reason? Just plain old fear. Because I had failed so much in my life, I unconsciously projected it into every new venture. Because of my mind-set, failure became inevitable.

Maybe we have tried and failed so many times that we no longer think victory is an option. The result is a self-fulfilling prophecy of defeat and failure. But if we can receive His life, we will find that He has never experienced failure. So He doesn't project it into life. That becomes freedom from fear for us.

SERVING IN NEWNESS

Even though our old life has been exchanged with the life of the Spirit of Christ, we still live in physical bodies that are weak in regard to our emotions and desires. John MacArthur reminds us: "Although Christians are not in the flesh, the flesh is still in us. We're no longer held captive to it, but we can still act fleshly or carnal."[12] In other words, we do not continue to sin because we are sin's slave; rather, we continue in disobedience because we still possess an unredeemed body that is susceptible to temptation.

As long as we live in our human bodies we will have to battle sin, particularly if we want to live outside the walls. Our only hope is to trust in the Spirit of Christ in us to live His life through us. He is perfectly comfortable, confident, and masterful in dealing with anything which your life throws at you. So all you have to do is allow Him to live through you.

His new life allows us to serve others joyfully, energetically, and effectively. Serving in the new life is not at all like serving in prison. We served in prison because it was an imposed punishment. We serve in the freedom of the Spirit because it bubbles up out of His life which flows through us. **"He came to serve" (Matthew 10:25)**, and now, He does that through the members of His Body in the earth.

Session 3 **The Exchange**

What do you think is the difference in serving according to the law and according to the Spirit?

Do you ever find yourself choosing the prison of the law rather than the freedom of the Spirit?

SIN'S OPPORTUNITY

"What should we say then? Is the law sin? Absolutely not! On the contrary, I would have not known sin if it were not for the law. For example, I would not have known what it is to covet if the law had not said, You shall not covet. And sin, seizing an opportunity through the commandment, produced in me coveting of every kind. For apart from the law sin is dead" (Romans 7: 7-8).

Up to this point, the law has been painted in a pretty negative light. So far we have called it a prison, a bad marriage, and a cruel taskmaster. But before we go too far and call it "sin", Paul steps in. Romans 7: 8 contains the astonishing thought: The holy law of God is not sin, but it sure gives sin an opportunity.

I have two precious daughters. At this writing, Evelyn is 4 years old. Naturally, I love her so much that it hurts. Sometimes, when I gaze at her sleeping or playing, I realize again how much she is undefiled by the world. Even so, the more I tell her not to do something, the more she wants to do it. Where does that come from in a 4-year-old girl?

Maybe it comes from the same place that gives rise to the overwhelming desire to rake your fingers across fresh paint—especially when there is a DO NOT TOUCH sign in front of it. When a federal law, city regulation, father's warning, or even a simple painter's sign identifies the forbidden act, it "arouses" our very desire to do it. Our sinful nature is a terrorist. It comes roaring out of the shadows and demands indulgence of our creature desires, even in a pure and innocent child or a casual passer of wet paint.

As we begin to understand the Bible and learn of God's righteous requirements, something in those requirements seems to energize our own inclination to disobey. Again, it's the "WET PAINT. DO NOT TOUCH" syndrome. So the law "Do not covet" suddenly provides an opportunity for sin to produce "coveting of every kind."

In many of us, that makes us try harder to control sin with our own strength. But that is fighting fire with gasoline. We end up flaming out in sin.

RUN TO HIM

In his book *Grace Rules*, Steven McVey says that . . . "Trying to overcome sin by changing one's behavior is typical of a person whose life is ruled by law. Remember that the law is a system whereby someone tries to make spiritual progress or gain God's blessings based on what he or she does. In a life where graces rules, victory over sin is experienced by the expression of the indwelling Christ within us."[13]

When we strive for righteousness *independent* of Jesus Christ living His life through ours, we are living under the law. We are like a broken branch of an apple tree, lying on the ground, trying to grow an apple.

After reading Romans 7:5, we are all tempted to think, "if the law arouses me to sin then isn't the law a bad thing?" No, not at all. The law—primarily the Ten Commandments—reflects God's perfection. It is a social as well as personal model of behavior. The problem arises when we try to make the law something it isn't. It is a reflection; it is not rebirth. It does not help, equip, or empower people.

You might say that the Lord gave us the law so that we would run as fast as we could to Him. He helps. He equips. He empowers. The law was never designed for those actions. The law reveals our need. But then we must run to Him for the response to the need. The law reveals our desperate situation; Jesus does something about it.

> Why do you think the law arouses our sinful desires?

> Is it a struggle for you to appreciate the law?

"Therefore, my brothers, you also were put to death in relation to the law through the crucified body of the Messiah, so that you may belong to another—to Him who was raised from the dead—that we may bear fruit for God." —Romans 7:4

🛒 Take Away

☐ Evaluate the relationships in your life. Do you accept people according to their identity or their behavior?

☐ Go back and re-read the giving of the law found in Exodus 19-20.

☐ Commit Romans 7:4 to memory.

Prayer

OH! DIVINE REDEEMER, out of whose inexhaustible fullness I would

daily draw a rich supply of grace into my needy soul,

Be pleased to impart unto me an undivided heart;

That to please You may be my greatest happiness,

Aand to promote Your glory my highest honor.

Preserve me from false motives,

From a double mind, and a divided heart.

Keep me entirely to Yourself,

And enable me to crucify every lust

Which would tempt my heart from You.

Enable me by Your grace to walk in one uniform path

Of holy, childlike obedience.

When tempted to turn aside to the right hand or to the left,

May I keep steadily Your way until, brought before Your throne,

I see Your face, behold Your smile, and fall in ecstasy at Your feet,

Lost in wonder, love, and praise.

THOMAS READE

Notes

Notes

SESSION 4

Exchanging Failure

WE DON'T OFTEN FACE the reality of our depravity. Our inability to do so is clearly visible in the way we present the gospel. As a Christian musician I have been involved with thousands of altar calls in my ministry journey. Many times I have heard a plea that goes something like, "Come to Christ and you will find joy and peace and a reason for living."

Although that is true, it is incomplete. It is only when we see the reality of our desperate situation that the gospel becomes the truly good news about redemption. One leader said, "You will never know grace until you *have* to have it." Of course, we cannot give people that revelation. God has a way of delivering the sobering reality of our condition. Flesh will eventually and inevitably hit the wall. When that happens, as we lie there bruised and bleeding, we suddenly see the absolute insufficiency of our best efforts and the stink of our flesh. At that point, we mutter, "Oh God, be merciful to me a sinner." Then redemption can begin.

If that moment has come in your life, you are an excellent candidate to fully embrace the exchanged life. The misery of your condition and the frustration of your inadequate will power can lead you to something better; it did for Paul . . . it has for me.

EXCHANGING FAILURE

ROMANS 7:9-25

FROM LAW TO LIFE

Throughout his ministry Paul was accused of preaching a message that permitted careless living because Christ's death on the cross had already paid any and all penalties of sin. These accusations came many times from people of a Jewish background who struggled to see how the law—what they had built their entire lives around—fit inside of Paul's gospel.

By Paul's day, Judaism had evolved into a religious system by which people had to earn their way into God's love by strict observance of and obedience to the law.

Joseph Girzone summarized that system very well in his book, *A Portrait of Jesus:*

> "At the time of Jesus, people were burdened with layer upon layer of laws that regulated the smallest detail of daily life. Besides the oppressive laws of their Roman conquerors, there was a body of Jewish law, civil and religious. And among the religious laws there were not just ten commandments. There were 613 commandments and 365 prohibitions, and many hundreds lesser injunctions that people had to follow. When they could not measure up to these ideals, the religious leaders excommunicated them and cut them off from the society . . . "[14]

As a Jew himself, Paul could appreciate his detractors intention of preserving the goodness of the law. But Paul also understood that the law was serving a role in Jewish culture that it was never meant to serve. For while the law is a reflection of the character of God, it does not offer the power to be conformed to that character. Empowerment to become conformed to God's image only came through Christ.

"Once I was alive apart from the law, but when the commandment came, sin sprang to life and I died. The commandment that was meant for life resulted in death for me" (Romans 7: 9-10).

A misreading of this text would suggest Paul considered himself as spiritually alive before he understood the law. I think Paul was only saying that he—who was highly educated in the law—was better at obeying the law than most people. He once wrote, **"If anyone else thinks he has grounds for confidence in the flesh, I have more" (Philippians 3:4)**.

Session 4 **The Exchange**

FROM REALITY TO REDEMPTION

Paul was on the dream team of Jewish leaders. He obeyed the law to the very last detail, at least in his mind. But we can see pretty clearly from Romans 7 that even Paul had an active sin life. As a legalist, he had been so focused on external behavior that he ignored his inner motives and desires. Of course, God's standard of righteousness reaches beyond action to motive.

Then one day Paul the Pharisee saw himself more accurately, and he was disintegrated by the recognition of his sinfulness. When Christ revealed Himself to Paul, he finally saw himself in the light of God's holiness.

Catching a glimpse of our own righteousness is a shattering experience. Compared to the character of God, we realize we are no good. We are permanently stained with the filth and slime of sin. Before we can ever move to redemption, we have to face reality.

"For sin seizing an opportunity through the commandment, deceived me, and through it killed me. So then, the law is holy, and the commandment is holy, and just and good" (Romans 7: 11-12).

The law is good at a lot of things. It is good at drawing boundaries and guidelines. It's good at establishing a basis for moral conduct. It's so good at these things that Judeo-Christian ethics are the foundation of law for most Western civilizations. But there are also things for which the law is completely unhelpful. For example, the law does not redeem.

Watch the video segment "From SanFran to O-o-o-o-klahoma" when you meet with your group to discussion this session. You'll learn a lot more about author Joel Engle's life and experiences.

We may read the law, appreciate it, and even have good intentions about our reaction to it. But at the end of the day, regardless of our intentions, our carnal nature is more powerful than our ability to obey. That is why we have societal systems of management and punishment: fines, rehab centers, community service, prisons, etc. Societies go to great effort and expense to constrain sinful behavior. But all those efforts can only restrict our evil actions; they can't change the heart. God's law can't either.

> Think of a time in your life when you were a grace abuser. What contributed to that abuse?
>
> How does living under the law appeal to you?

IT IS WHAT IT IS

Nevertheless, living under the law is appealing to us. Maybe that's because it gives us a role in our own righteousness, and something in our makeup wants part of the process we can claim as our own. Let's face it; the prophet was accurate when he said that our righteous acts are no better than filthy rags (Isaiah 64:6).

"Therefore, did what is good cause my death? Absolutely not! On the contrary, sin, in order to be recognized as sin, was producing death in me through what is good, so that through the commandment sin might become sinful beyond measure" (Romans 7:13).

Paul is saying here that sin is what destroys us, and the law is what defines sin as sin. The law provides the absolute boundary markers making sin and righteousness black and white issues. It serves as a huge spotlight shining on our sinful nature and the power of sin.

As that light, the law illuminates our sinful behaviors and catches us red-handed. It doesn't cause us to sin, but it sure does a great job of revealing it. Even when we are not caught in the act, it still reveals our sinful nature.

Let's be careful though. Paul did not criticize the law and neither should we. It is good, but it is what it is. It's not the focus of the Christian life; it only reveals our weakness. Christ should be our only focus. You don't drive by looking at the ditches; you see them out of the corner of your eye while making sure your focus is straight ahead. As simple as that sounds, it is actually very contradictory to the current Christian culture.

According to that culture, Christians are to not lust, curse, get angry, lie or "be bad." However, real, abundant life cannot be defined or lived according to the "not's". The Christian life is about a relationship of love with Christ.

Can you imagine using a computer to cut your grass? How about downloading your e-mail using a weed-eater? That sounds crazy doesn't it? You need to use the correct tools for the appropriate job. The law is a tool. It defines and illustrates sin. It is not the power tool for the Christian life. Christ Himself is the perfect and only instrument for living that life.

That is why we need to realize and internalize that we have a new life in Him through His finished work at Calvary. The cross really did make the difference. We now have a new nature that longs for God and is empowered with the Holy Spirit. That is God's method for living. That is the exchanged life.

WEAKNESS AND POWER

Despite the number of years I've been walking with the Lord, I continue to stumble and fall. Sometimes it seems that I crash and burn on a daily basis. Sure, there are days when I am better able to release Christ to be the power of my life, but there are also days when I move in ways that are independent of Him. Like everyone trying to follow Christ, I hate my inconsistency and get very frustrated with my weakness.

It is somewhat reassuring to know that the apostle Paul struggled the same way. That is part of what I love about the Bible. It doesn't hide anything about the heroes of our faith. So in his great book of Romans, Paul—perhaps the greatest theologian of all time—reveals that at times he was weak just like the rest of us. Paul was just a human being with the same weaknesses, hang-ups, and weirdness that we all feel from time to time.

Paul once wrote that he **"boasts in his weaknesses" (2 Corinthians 12:9)**. In the same verse, he went on to explain that his weaknesses allowed the power of Christ to dwell in him. Weakness and failure are not causes for rejection by God; they release His power to flow through us.

"For we know that the law is spiritual; but I am made out of flesh, sold into sin's power. For I do not understand what I am doing, because I do not practice what I want to do, but I do what I hate" (Romans 7: 14-15).

I really do love God's law. Before I knew Christ, I couldn't have possibly cared less. But now I love to consider the holiness of God and His perfect law. They are beautiful to me now that I am redeemed from the authority and reach of sin.

However, as a human being, I am unable to obey the law even though I love it. Why? Because my emotions, physical desires, and general human weaknesses are just not good enough. That is why I am so desperate for Christ's power to live through me. You see, my weakness releases His strength. His strength bears His spiritual fruit through me. Just like the apple branch is dependent on the roots, trunk, and whole creative circle of life, I can produce fruit as His life rises in my branches.

THE FRUIT OF THE SPIRIT

Paul said that **"the fruit of the Spirit is love, joy, peace, patience, kindness, goodness, faith, gentleness, and self-control" (Galatians 5:22-23)**.

Regarding this verse, Martin Luther wrote, "The righteous has no need of any law to admonish or to constrain him; without constraint of the law, he willingly does those things which the law requires. Therefore, the law cannot accuse and condemn those who believe in Christ."[15]

Since we have a new nature in Christ, our hearts are set on Him. All of the love, joy, peace, etc., that we will ever need are found in Him. He does the fruit-bearing when we depend upon Him.

"And if I do what I do not want to do, I agree with the law that it is good. So now I am no longer the one doing it, but it is sin living in me" (Romans 7: 16-17).

I sometimes cringe when I read verses like these. I guess I just wish that Paul sounded more victorious. Here, in the life of the great apostle, the ferocious and often painful battle against sin is visible for all to see. It's hard to look at someone considered to be such a giant of the faith and see these struggles.

Pastor John MacArthur says this about the side of Paul visible in these verses: "You know what kind of Christian this is? My friend, this is the most mature spiritual Christian there could ever be who sees so clearly the inability of his flesh ... against the holiness of the divine standard. You see? And the more mature he is, and the more spiritual he is, the greater will be the sensitivity of his own shortcomings."[16]

Listen to the audio file "When Life Needs a 'Do-over'" as you study this session. Think about the last time you wished you could rewind your life.

If that is true, then maturity is not so much defined as strength and independence, but weakness and dependence. Paul said as much in another of his writings: **"I will most gladly boast all the more about my weaknesses, so that Christ's power may reside in me. So because of Christ, I am pleased in weaknesses, in insults, in catastrophes, in persecutions, and in pressures. For when I am weak, then I am strong" (2 Corinthians 12:9-10).**

I believe a mark of Paul's Christian maturity can be seen in his absolute clarity about the source of his strength. When he writes about not practicing what he wants to do and about sin operating through him, he is simply recognizing that human nature is never good enough. If you look to it for your strength, you will end up humiliated. If, on the other hand, you face your own weaknesses, you will find that the superior life of Christ comes roaring through them to fill you with a new kind of strength. It is only then, in our weakness, that we find true strength.

Is it difficult for you to boast in your weaknesses?

What holds you back from that ability?

Session 4 **The Exchange**

THE BATTLE

One of my favorite parts of *The Matrix* is when Morpheus presents Neo with two pills. One will lead him back to blissful ignorance; the other will take him into a painful reality. Neo chooses the reality pill. That choice is hard, but clearly the right one.

Reality is always our friend. Someone said that before we can become disillusioned, we must first have an illusion. Well, it's an illusion to think the Christian life is one of bliss, ease, and happy ignorance. The Lord, in His great mercy, is always faithful to bring us to the end of that illusion. In reality, walking out the Christian life here on earth is a struggle. More accurately, it is a war.

Most of the wars in history were fought over real estate. The spiritual war is no different; the real estate in question is the land between our ears—our minds. Paul said that we have the mind of Christ (1 Corinthians 2:16), and it's true: we do have a new spirit-man dwelling inside of us. He is holy, righteous, and longs to please the heart of God. Unfortunately, our earthly self also fights for its own rights and territories.

BETWEEN THE PROMISE AND THE DITCH

"By these He has given us very great and precious promises, so that through them you may share in the divine nature, escaping the corruption that is in the world because of evil desires" (2 Peter 1:4).

The battle inside of us rages between heaven and earth. On the one hand, we have all of God's promises to count on each day. On the other hand, we are stuck in a body that is made out of dirt and seems to always be inclined toward the earthy. We are somewhat like a car out of alignment. Take your hand off the wheel, and it drifts toward the ditch.

Have evil thoughts ever come flooding into your mind while you were praying? Scary, isn't it? You probably wondered, "How in the world can I be a Christian and have those kinds of thoughts running around in my head?" We have all the promises and truths of God coexisting with the problems and gutters of sin. It's sometimes difficult to steer between the two.

"For I know that nothing good lives in me, that is, in my flesh. For the desire to do what is good is with me, but there is no ability to do it. For I do not do the good that I want to do, but I practice the evil that I do not want to do" (Romans 7: 18-19).

Paul said, " . . . nothing good lives in me, that is, in my flesh." In his human flesh, the great Hebrew of Hebrews was a weak and inadequate man, vulnerable to sin. Paul was not surprised or ashamed of his own inadequacies. He knew how to face reality.

Paul knew that the weakness and corruption in his flesh was part of the package of living in a body. Just as he was not surprised or embarrassed about perspiration, bad breath, exhaustion, or an inability to leap tall buildings in a single bound, he knew that flesh is flesh. Flesh will never be adequate for the ascension to higher places.

RUBBER BAND FAITH

A few years ago, a visiting minister told the men in my home church that they should wear a rubber band around their wrist. Every time they had a lustful thought, they should pull the band away from their wrist and let it go. Ouch!

That is like taking a paper clip to a knife fight. You cannot join the spiritual battle with a rubber band attempt at behavior modification. It was a Christ-less solution for an issue which only Christ can touch. Jesus' solution for lust or any other creature condition is found in John 15:5: **"I am the vine; you are the branches. The one who remains in Me and I in him produces much fruit, because you can do nothing without Me."**

"Now if I do what I do not want, I am no longer the one doing it, but it is the sin that lives in me. So I discover this principle: when I want to do good, evil is with me" (Romans 7: 20-21).

We have a choice between two, and only two, options. Rubber bands or the power of the vine.

We can allow sin to reign or Christ to reign. It is really that simple. Paul says something very similar to this in **Galatians 5:17. "For the flesh desires what is against the Spirit, and the Spirit desires what is against the flesh; these are opposed to each other, so that you don't do what you want."**

Whenever we step onto the battlefield for Christ, we should expect sin to be crouching there, poised for attack. Don't go out there armed with rubber bands. Go there with the arsenal of the power of God flowing through you, confident in who Christ is and who He has made you to be.

What are some ways you can develop a war-time mentality?

Listen to "Into Your Arms" by Matt Papa. (It's on your *Exchange* playlist.) Matt's pretty honest about his struggles. In what ways do you relate to his lyrics?

Session 4 **The Exchange**

How can you be prepared for the attack from sin without dwelling on sin?

OVERNIGHT SUCCESS

When I was I kid, I loved comic books. Spiderman, Superman, Batman, Aquaman, and the Green Lantern were my favorites. From the back of those comic books, cheesy advertisements promised wonderful and exotic adventures. Who wouldn't want the pet rock, the joy buzzer, sea monkeys, and all that other great stuff?

One of those ads enticed me into purchasing the body-building secrets of Charles Atlas. The ad promised that I would have an Atlas body in seven days! Charles Atlas was the guy who coined the phrase "ninety-seven pound weakling." That was me.

I worked out with the Atlas exercises faithfully. Every day, all day long, I did them. Seven days later, I was still a skinny little kid. I tried harder and harder. Nothing. I was still a skinny, scrawny seventh-grade wimp.

There is no overnight fox to become like Jesus, and there is no amount of work you can do in your own strength to conform yourself to Him. He has given you and me everything we need in Him. He is willing to live His life through ours, but receiving His life is an act of moment-by-moment faith, trust, and dependence upon His power working through us.

"For in my inner self I joyfully agree with God's law. But I see a different law in the parts of my body, waging war against the law of my mind and taking me prisoner to the law of sin in the parts of my body" (Romans 7: 22-23).

BEYOND PASSIVITY

After reading this far, you may have the impression that serving God is passive. Since Christ has done all we need, we are free to just step back and let His life come roaring through us. Right?

His strength is sufficient and empowering, but life is far from passive. Paul told his friends in Corinth, **"But by God's grace I am what I am, and His grace toward me was not ineffective. However, *I worked more than any of them*, yet not I, but God's grace that was in me" (1 Corinthians 15:10, emphasis added).**

Part of the purpose of the spiritual war being fought within us is to strengthen our condition. Our "workouts" against forces that would take us prisoner are far more beneficial than the Charles Atlas course. Through the struggle, spiritual muscles are formed that we need for the real work ahead. We must remember that those workouts are only effective if they come from Christ in us.

The grace of God makes us what we are; we are not responsible or credited with it at all. That grace builds a platform from which we are released to work very hard. In fact, Paul said that he worked harder than anyone else.

The grace of God has qualified us to join with the Lord in His great work. Think of it—the war which wages within our own mind and body is a gym in which we become qualified to partner with God in the great and thrilling work of extending His reign throughout the earth.

If you read through Matthew, Mark, Luke, John, and Acts., you'll see how *active* they are. People—empowered by His grace—were in continual motion. Sailing on great waters, *walking* on great waters, climbing mountains, healing the sick, joining with Jesus to miraculously feed large gatherings . . . these were busy and hard-working people.

Paul was an energetic, aggressive, servant of God. He was very clear about operating in the strength of God, but doing so in great work. He told the Corinthians: **"For although we are walking in the flesh, we do not wage war in a fleshly way, since the weapons of our warfare are not fleshly, but are powerful through God for the demolition of strongholds. We demolish arguments and every high-minded thing that is raised up against the knowledge of God, taking every thought captive to the obedience of Christ" (2 Corinthians 10:3-5).**

That is not the statement of a pacifist.

"WRETCHED?"

"What a wretched man I am! Who will rescue me from this body of death? I thank God through Jesus Christ our Lord! So then, with my mind I myself am a slave to the law of God, but with my flesh, to the law of sin" (Romans 7: 24-25).

Paul's use of the word *wretched* used to really mess me up. How could Paul talk in some places about his strength through Christ and freedom from sin and the law and still call himself wretched?

Session 4 **The Exchange**

We think of wretched as a synonym for "wicked", but the word is more accurately understood as "afflicted" or "distressed." I don't think this statement is one of self-deprecation; I think these are the words from a man weary after hard work. Paul is looking at the limitations of his flesh and wishing he could be free of that easily-exhausted, smelly, and failing body. Then he could do some real work.

Then his mind realizes the answer to the question he just asked. Jesus Christ our Lord is the very One Who enables us to work outside our own afflicted and distressed body. After arriving at that inspired thought, I think Paul was probably ready to go on into further work—joyful work.

I meet a lot of miserable, unhappy Christians. Most of them don't even know that they are miserable because they have become used to the state of failure and weariness in their spiritual journey. Part of their unhappiness is related to passivity. Indulging your own creature comforts is one sure slide into depression. Want to get really down in the dumps? Try watching TV or surfing the Internet or eating all day.

If you want to get out of yourself, go help someone. If you want to escape despair and depression, throw yourself into serving. Nothing is more therapeutic than working hard—as a member of Christ's body in the earth.

How do grace and work fit together?

How do you think God feels when you work for Him?

"Now if I do what I do not want, I am no longer the one doing it, but it is the sin that lives in me."
— Romans 7:20

⛟ Take Away

☐ As you struggle with sin this week, try thanking God for this reminder that the Holy Spirit lives in you.
☐ Do some online research about some of the different views of Romans 7.
☐ Commit Romans 7:20 to memory.

Prayer

OH GOD, I have tasted Thy goodness
And it has both satisfied me and made me thirsty for more.
I am painfully conscious of my need of further grace;
I am ashamed of my lack of desire.
O God, the Triune God, I want to want Thee;
I long to be filled with longing;
I thirst to be made more thirsty still.
Show me Thy glory,
I pray Thee, so that I may know Thee indeed.
Begin in mercy a new work of love within me.
Say to my soul, "Rise up, my love, my fair one, and come away."
Then give me grace to rise and follow Thee
Up from this misty lowland where I have wandered so long.

A.W. TOZIER

Notes

SESSION 5

Exchanging Effort

I RECENTLY WATCHED a documentary about a man facing execution. The program painted a fine portrait of his fear, the fight to overturn his sentence, and in the end, his death.

I cannot imagine living on a prison's death row. Having a sentence of death hanging over your head must be one of the heaviest burdens ever experienced by anyone. It is much weightier than just facing your end. The real weight of the death sentence is the knowledge that you have been forever marked guilty and that you are not considered fit to remain in human society.

Many followers of Jesus Christ still carry a secret fear that God may still hold them accountable for their sins and mistakes. Somewhere, in the back of their mind, they fear that God has a death sentence still waiting for them. This private dread keeps them from enjoying the very real love of God in their daily experience.

Exchanging Effort

ROMANS 8:1-15

FULL PARDON

"Therefore, no condemnation now exists for those in Christ Jesus" (Romans 8:1).

Can you even imagine the bursting joy of relief at being fully pardoned from a death sentence? Let those words—"No condemnation now exists for those in Christ Jesus"—wash over your heart. You once had a death sentence, but now you will never perish. You are free to walk away from death row and into life.

What Jesus did on the cross for us has now set us free from the just and righteous condemnation of God. I am continually saddened that so many believers continue to live in fear of God's judgment. Are they just not paying attention? Why would they choose to dwell in fear about their future? As tragic and perplexing as that is, I do understand it. I carried the same fear for a long time in my life.

You have been forgiven and are released from all condemnation. That means that hell is absolutely out of the equation, but His pardon does even more than that. Peter wrote that you have been **"redeemed from your empty way of life inherited from the fathers . . . " (1 Peter 1:18).**

Because of the severity of the curse on Adam and Eve, all of the earth and humanity fell into a futile way of life. Life was a pointless, empty, wasted, and unproductive exercise. It still is for those who do not know Christ.

However, when Jesus went to the cross and spilled out His life, he redeemed us—bought us back—from that empty life which had prevailed throughout all the generations from Adam. Now, we no longer have to live a futile and barren life. We are free to from that vicious cycle of death and emptiness.

"Because the Spirit's law of life in Christ Jesus has set you free from the law of sin and of death" (Romans 8:2).

FREE TO LIVE

Do you understand? Do you get it? Christ, the Lion-Lamb, the Servant-Warrior, faced sin and death on the cross, and purchased *your* life. He walked into the slave-market

Session 5 **The Exchange**

of history and said, "I'll take that one! And, that one … and, that one, and … you." He bought you back and rescued you from the abuse of the slave master.

Here's the way John described that purchase: **"Paying in blood, you bought men and women, bought them back from all over the earth, bought them back for God" (Revelation 5:9, *The Message*).**

We still fail. We still, at times, lust for pleasure. We still lie at times. We still harbor anger and resentment for people who hurt us. We still get full of ourselves and become arrogant and ignore the power of Christ's life to live through us. Yet even in the middle of all of our weaknesses, we can rest assured that God will forgive us because we have been placed in the love of Jesus Christ.

Remember—since He bought you, He owns you. You no longer belong to yourself. **"He has rescued us from the domain of darkness and transferred us into the kingdom of the Son He loves, in whom we have redemption, the forgiveness of sins" (Colossians 1:13-14).**

> What holds you back from having complete assurance in your relationship with God?

> How should the truth of Romans 8:1-2 change the way you practically live?

A NEW HEART

Louie Giglio looked at his Bible and then asked those of us gathered for the youth pastor's conference. "How many of you think the Christian life is hard?" Immediately, our hands reached for the ceiling. We waited for the approval of our teacher.

"Wrong," Louie announced. Hands sank to laps. "The Christian life is not hard; it is impossible. You can't do it; only Christ can."

That day, my theology came crashing into the ground of truth. Louie was right. The Christian life is impossible. In our weak and sin-battered human state, we have no natural resistance to sin. We can no more live out the spiritual principles of the Bible in our own strength than a 3-year-old child can fly an airplane.

The law of God tells us what we are to do and what we are not to do, but it can't give us the power to carry out our behavior. God didn't leave us hanging out to dry though. According to Paul, **"He [God] made the One [Jesus] who did not know sin to be sin for us, so that we might become the righteousness of God in Him" (2 Corinthians 5:21, parenthesis added).**

Session 5 **Exchanging Effort**

"What the law could not do since it was limited by the flesh, God did. He condemned sin in the flesh by sending His own Son in flesh like ours under sin's domain, and as a sin offering" (Romans 8:3).

God didn't send an angel, a prophet, a king, or a celebrity to overcome the power of sin against His children. He sent His own Son, Jesus Christ. His sacrifice dealt with the power of sin once and for all.

Ray Stedman explained it this way, ". . . somehow the Lord Jesus, at the hour of darkness, gathered up all the sins of the world, all the terrible, evil, foul, awful injustice, crime, and misery that we have seen throughout history, from every person, gathered it into himself, and brought it to an end by dying. The good news is that somehow, by faith in him, we get involved in that death."[17]

INVITED INTO HIM

We are privileged to be a part of Christ's death and resurrection. We died to sin and have been made alive to God forever. We must get this into our heads and hearts if we are going to experience the exchanged life.

God doesn't want you and me to live any more on our own power, trusting in our instincts and conventional wisdom. God has invited us out of that. We are no longer left to our own self-indulgent living; we have been invited to experience Christ-dependent living. We are called unto Jesus.

"In order that the law's requirement would be met in us who do not walk according to the flesh but according to the Spirit" (Romans 8:4).

In this verse, Paul declares that all the law required has now been satisfied in Christ. Even further, that success—His success—is imparted to and realized in us according to the initiative and power of the Spirit. Now we are free to lead a new life.

"I WILL CAUSE YOU TO WALK . . ."

In that sense, Romans 8:3–4 is a New Testament version of Ezekiel 36:26-27: **"I will give you a new heart and put a new spirit within you; I will remove your heart of stone and give you a heart of flesh. I will place My Spirit within you and cause you to follow My statutes and carefully observe My ordinances."**

In other words, we don't have to meticulously try to follow words on stone or paper; He has placed His Spirit within us, and that Spirit becomes transfused into our own lives. As a result, we obey because it is His (and now *our*) nature to do so.

Session 5 **The Exchange**

Our new life is an active working relationship with the God of the universe.

We live in rather sedentary times; we sit a lot. We sit at our computers, in staff meetings, on airplanes, in Starbucks, and in conferences. Because of the nature of our information economy, sometimes we are accomplishing real work when we sit.

I suggest that you read through the Bible with an eye toward the activity. The Bible features people in the midst of great adventures. Don't let the sedentary nature of our times and our economy lull you into thinking like spectators. Walking in new life is a cooperative, engaging, global adventure of joining together in the unfolding of the Kingdom of God.

Do you realize that today, Muslims are embracing Christ? Underground churches are changing the direction of nations, and large movements of Christ-followers are feeding the hungry in the world's most poverty-stricken areas. Christian leaders are forming partnerships which are doing more in the AIDS crisis than the programs and funding of whole nations.

All of this is happening because of the freedom and power which Christ unlocked on the cross. He now *causes* us to walk in His heart and attitude toward the world. Isn't it time for you to sign up? Wanna know how?

What are some practical ways you can tap into the power of Jesus in a moment-by-moment fashion?

Is your life characterized by sitting or walking?

THE TWO-WAY ROAD

Success and failure both begin with attitude. Winning athletes and teams have winning attitudes. Many businesses fail because they don't have the correct mind-set and corporate culture for success. One of the effects of **"the futile way of life inherited from our forefathers" (I Peter 1:18)** is that many choose an attitude which dooms them to failure.

Paul says in Romans 8:5 that our mind is either set on "the things of the flesh" or "the things of the Spirit." No other choice is possible. If we choose the flesh, we will always live in sensuality, conflict, and defeat. If we choose the Spirit, we will live on the higher plane of eternity, walking through life as God's ambassadors to the earth.

How do you think Jesus walked through the earth? Do you think he chose the flesh? Of course not. He could walk through any situation—like community leaders preparing to stone an adulterous woman, or the death of a friend, or money changers in the temple, or even a midnight stroll on the lake—because He always kept Heaven on his sights.

Jesus said that He only did on earth what pleased His Father (John 8:28). And as Paul wrote, **"Your attitude should be the same as that of Christ Jesus" (Phil. 2:5).** In other words, we can dial into the same God-to-earth frequency Jesus listened to.

"For those whose lives are according to the flesh think about the things of the flesh, but those whose lives are according to the Spirit, about the things of the Spirit. For the mind-set of the flesh is death, but the mind-set of the Spirit is life and peace. For the mind-set of the flesh is hostile to God because it does not submit itself to God's law, for it is unable to do so. Those whose lives are in the flesh are unable to please God" (Romans 8:5-8).

The battle against sin and death begins and ends in our minds. Remember we have the power to either choose life or death (Deuteronomy 30:19). By our choice of mind-set, we can decide which channel to keep tuned in.

INWARD OR OUTWARD?

While ministering at a youth camp in Panama City Beach, Florida, I drove back to my lodging to get some rest between services. As I waited for the light to change near the beach, I saw the whole panorama of life of the flesh as described by Paul in Galatians 5:19-21. **"Now the works of the flesh are obvious: sexual immorality, moral impurity, promiscuity, idolatry, sorcery, hatreds, strife, jealousy, outbursts of anger, selfish ambitions, dissensions, factions, envy, drunkenness, carousing, and anything similar."**

Have you ever noticed that the flesh life always pulls us inward? It makes life about *me.* That kind of attitude causes people to assume that all of life should bow down to them and their desires. In contrast, life in the spirit pulls us outward into service toward others, pouring out our life for a greater and higher purpose, sacrificing our personal preferences for the good of someone else.

If you read stories about history's great Christ-followers, you will consistently find an outward focus characterizing their lives. From George Washington Carver to Mother Teresa to Billy Graham, they all knew that life was not about, or for, themselves.

Session 5 **The Exchange**

The movie *End of the Spear* is the incredible, true adventure of Jim Elliot, Nate Saint, Roger Youderian, Pete Fleming, and Ed McCully. These five missionaries were savagely murdered by the Waodani tribe in Ecuador. In response to the tragedy, their widows and children immediately followed in their path. Many moved to live near the tribe. As a result, the tribe embraced Christ. The vicious and multi-generational cycle of a futile way of life stopped. Today the same men who speared the missionaries are elders of the church in that region.

WHAT ABOUT YOU?

Do you think these kinds of bold acts are only accessible by super saints? Think again. Consider T.W. Hunt's words in his book, *The Mind of Christ*: "You must set your mind. You must decide, choose, or determine the focus of your mind. That is where you start in developing the mind of Christ. The opposite of the will is instinct or unwilled reactions . . . The will enables you to obey in spite of your feelings or intuitions."[18]

If you can step out of yourself and give your whole being to Christ, then you too can start living an outward-focused life. That doesn't mean we should ignore our own heart—far from it. Because of the exchange, we receive the life of Christ. That means at our core, our heart beats in rhythm with the heart of Jesus. It's up to us to embrace His life that lives inside of us. We can do that only through consistent practice ad deliberate intention. Much of maturity is the process of developing what has already been implanted in us. Or, as John suggested, it is about decreasing so that Jesus and His mind can increase (John 3:30).

His mind is always toward the world He died for. Now His Body (which includes you) is moving according to His mind. Therefore, our life purpose should be swallowed up in the **"kind intention of His will." (Ephesians 1:5)**.

> What are some practical ways you can battle for Christ's control of your mind?

> Why, in your opinion, is the real estate of the mind so vital for spiritual victory?

THE SWEET LIFE

Recently, after my daily jog, I walked into my house, and saw Elizabeth playing on the floor. I needed a shower, but since I am a 4-year-old at heart, I dropped to the floor and began to play with her. "Daddy!" she shrieked, "You stink!" I was shattered.

After all, I "stunk" because I was trying to stay in shape and be healthy. Did she not have any appreciation for all my hard work?

I think we would be surprised to know how our spiritual sweat smells to God. We seem to have the attitude that our sweat is a pleasing aroma in His nostrils. However, the sweat we produce from all our good works still smells terrible to God. He isn't interested in our perspiration. He wants us to exchange our sweat for the sweetness of His life.

If we are really **"hidden in Christ" (Colossians 3:3)**, then the bad things we've done don't count against us and the good things we've done don't count for us. It is all about Him, not us.

Human life is only triumphant when it is lived by, in, and for Him. There are two kinds of Christian faith. One is found in the Bible. The other is a folk religion created by our culture. The former one is about life poured out for the higher call of Christ. The latter one is man-centered. Sadly, that is the one which seems to carry more influence in our postmodern era.

The old prophet Jeremiah delivered a profound truth when he said, **"I know, Lord, that a man's way of life is not his own; no one who walks determines his own steps" (Jeremiah 10:23)**. It's foolish to ever assume that a good or successful life can be found within ourselves. Looking for it within ourselves is like searching for words of wisdom on MTV. Let's face it. We don't know how to walk through life. We didn't create it, so we don't know how it really works.

By dying to any illusion that we are sufficient, by yielding it all over to Him, we can discover real life. The superior life of Christ will actually live in us.

"You, however, are not in the flesh, but in the Spirit, since the Spirit of God lives in you. But if anyone does not have the Spirit of Christ, he does not belong to Him" (Romans 8:9).

YOU ARE A SANCTUARY

Is the Holy Spirit of Christ living in you? Going to church, believing in God, or respecting the Bible doesn't make you a true Christian. Being nice to others, giving money to missions, and listening to worship CDs doesn't mean that you are a true believer in Jesus Christ. The true mark of salvation is that the Holy Spirit of God lives within you.

The awareness of His constant presence frees us from a rigorous and overcautious life because the Holy Spirit teaches us, and convicts us of error. He doesn't let us drift into sin without warning. He will gently nudge us away from the pitfalls of error. What an astonishing benefit of walking in the Spirit. **"Don't you know that you are God's sanctuary and that the Spirit of God lives in you?" (1 Corinthians 3:16).**

If He lives within you, then that makes you a temple of God. That means He—not you—is the Presence inside your life. When other people come to the temple that is Joel, they should encounter the presence of God's Spirit, not me. As John said, "I must decrease, so that He can increase."

"Now if Christ is in you, the body is dead because of sin, but the Spirit is life because of righteousness" (Romans 8:10).

AN INTEGRATED LIFE

In my years traveling within church circles, I have noticed that many Christians have built a compartmentalized life. They open one compartment for church services, conferences, camps, or concerts but live out of another compartment for their jobs, relationships, finances, hobbies, and entertainment.

To live like that is schizophrenic; it's fractured. Because He lives within us, we are free to live a wholly integrated life. In fact, I think integrated living is only possible if Christ lives in us. This is what the Christ-walk is all about: Christ functioning fully as the Lord over our thought life, jobs, relationships, hobbies, humor, speech, and family life.

"And if the Spirit of Him who raised Jesus from the dead lives in you, then He who raised Christ from the dead will also bring your mortal bodies to life through His Spirit who lives in you" (Romans 8:11).

RESURRECTION POWER

In Romans 8:11, Paul is not talking about the resurrection of the dead that will happen in the future; he is talking about resurrection life right now.

When I came to the end of myself and cried out to Jesus to take over my life, I died. I died to my own strengths, weaknesses, successes, failures, hopes, fears, and dreams. I faced the reality that I did not know how to walk in my own life.

It was over. The one who used to be known as Joel is now dead. Lay his dead carcass down in the grave. Bring in the dirt and pile it on top, because that old guy is gone. The one who is raised up is a resurrected new person.

Listen to the audio file "Thirsting After God" as you study this session. Think about the meaning of Psalm 63:1 in your life.

I have seen my marriage transformed by the power of Jesus Christ. I may not be the greatest husband in the world, but that's not the point. Because I died and a new Christ-life was resurrected in me, Valerie has a fine husband; my marriage reflects that new man. I'm not a great musician, but God has moved into my musical talent and communication abilities and used my life to impact thousand of others. If resurrection life has shown up in me, it will show up in anyone who comes to the end of themselves and invites Him to take up residence.

Have you given up? Are you at the end of yourself? Then, tell him. Invite Him to live in you and push you on out of the way. Resurrection life can be a way of life for you.

> Do you see death and resurrection happening in your life?

> Would you characterize your life as compartmentalized or integrated?

THE REAL WAR

I love a good war movie. It's not the blood or bullets but rather the pathos of human drama that pulls me in like a laser beam. The way people endure hardships, love their fellow soldiers, and fully commit to the cause is so inspiring. When I see or read about soldiers doing their duty in dangerous and life-threatening situations, I always wonder how I would behave in the same place.

One of my favorite heroes is Major Richard Winters of the 101st Airborne. This World War II veteran's life was made famous by the book and TV series, *Band of Brothers*. Major Winters was a hero's hero, an officer who led by example and put himself in harm's way over and over again in order to spare the lives of his men. In one of many battles that he and E company (of the 506 PIR) fought, Major Winters ran across an open field several hundred yards ahead of his men and attacked two companies of German soldiers. He risked his own life because he believed so deeply in what he was doing.

Revelation 12 tells the story of that war which broke out in heaven and now continues here on earth. We can live in—and daily apply—the victory of heaven over Satan and his realm, or we can live in a way that grants Satan a power that exists only by intimidation. In other words, we can let him bluff us into defeat.

In Revelation, John gave the plan for winning the war: **"They conquered him by the blood of the Lamb, and by the word of their testimony, for they did not love their lives in the face of death" (Revelation 12:11).**

When we love our own lives too much, we are not fit for His kingdom. That is what

Jesus meant when He said, **"whoever wants to save his life will lose it, but whoever loses his life because of Me will find it"** (Matthew 16:25).

"So then, brothers, we are not obligated to the flesh to live according to the flesh, for if you live according to the flesh, you are going to die. But if by the Spirit you put to death the deeds of the body, you will live. All those led by God's Spirit are God's sons" (Romans 8:12-14).

Paul clearly understood and embraced the dying to live principle. If we live according to the flesh, we will die. If we die to our own selfishness, we will live. When He lives within us and gives us a glimpse of the real war, we will stop giving in to our lusts, tempers, pride, selfish ambitions, greed, and insecurities. To live like this is a denial of what Christ has accomplished on the cross. He died that we might live. Now we live to, in, and for Him. Having laid down our own lives, we are free to be heroic soldiers.

WHERE DOES COURAGE COME FROM?

When I consider heroes like Major Richard Winters, I often wonder where that kind of courage comes from. Are you born with it? Do you learn it? Does the military have a way of instilling it? I think Paul gives the key in Romans 8:15.

"You did not receive a spirit of slavery to fall back into fear, but you received the Spirit of adoption, by whom we cry out, 'Abba, Father!'" (Romans 8:15).

Courage is found in the fatherhood of God. He said that we have not received a spirit of slavery which pulls us into fear, but rather we have been adopted by Father God. He has freed us from the power (and penalty) of sin, and has adopted us as His own. He will not leave us out in the cold. We can cry out to Him when we are tempted. He loves us and is more committed to our growth and spiritual maturity than we are. He will always lead us to victory if we will just trust Him. In other words, He imparts His own courage to us.

FATHERHOOD AND CONFIDENCE

Simply by knowing Him as our Father, we download His character. Knowing your father imparts confidence. As always, Jesus is our pattern here. **"Jesus knew that the Father had given everything into His hands, that He had come from God, and that He was going back to God. So He got up from supper, laid aside His robe, took a towel, and tied it around Himself. Next, He poured water into a basin and began to wash His disciples' feet and to dry them with the towel tied around Him"** (John 13:3-5).

Because Jesus was absolutely sure about His Father, He was free to serve. Think about that. Being established in your identity releases you to serve others sacrificially.

You may say, "But, Joel, I don't even know who my father is." I understand; I don't either. Look past that man (whoever he is) and behold your Heavenly Father. God will always be larger and more significant in your life than your own earthly father.

Elizabeth, my oldest daughter, is seriously afraid of thunder. Recently, a storm passed over our home and woke her from a nap. She came running to me, crying, "Daddy, the thunder scares me. Will you hold me?" I couldn't pick her up fast enough. As I held her, I began to sing a song that I wrote for her when she was born:

I love you, I love you, I love you I do
I love you, I love you, I love you I do
I love you, I love you,
I love you Elizabeth, you know it's true

She was soon asleep in her Daddy's arms. The love and security of Dad is enough to give us confidence in the storm.

No matter who you are, your heavenly Father loves you more than you can ever know. In the storms of your life, He quietly sings over you an eternal song of His infinite love for you, His child. You can run to Him when the thunder startles you.

What holds you back from embracing God as Father?

Do you have a need for courage in your life, or do you make choices according to preserving safety?

Take Away

- [ ] Plan a viewing of *The Passion of the Christ* with some people in your community in order to have a visual representation of the gospel.
- [ ] Leave an absent chair for Jesus at the dinner table this week to remind you that He experienced all of the common human needs like hunger.
- [ ] Commit Romans 8:1 to memory.

"Therefore, no condemnation now exists for those in Christ Jesus."
— Romans 8:1

Prayer

GIVE ME YOURSELF, O my God, give yourself to me.
Behold I love you, and if my love is too weak a thing,
Grant me to love you more strongly.
I cannot measure my love
To know how much it falls short of being sufficient,
But let my soul hasten to your embrace
And never be turned away until it is hidden
In the secret shelter of your presence.
This only do I know,
That it is not good for me when you are not with me,
When you are only outside me.
I want you in my very self.
All the plenty in the world which is not my God is utter want.
Amen.

ST. AUGUSTINE

Notes

Notes

SESSION 6

Exchanging Eternity

WHEN I WAS SIXTEEN I was battling great insecurities about my eternal destination and safety. Although I led what appeared to be a "normal" Christian life, I was in emotional agony.

One day I finally opened up and shared my struggles with Mom Engle. In response she just looked at me in great love and intensity, and said, "Joel, there are a lot of things you can doubt, but you can't go on doubting whether you know Christ or not. You don't mess with eternity."

She was right, of course. A few weeks later, I settled it once and for all time. In a defining moment, I came to believe that what He did on the cross was enough to remove the corruption and power of sin from my life.

Are you secure in your relationship with Christ? If not, I can only pass Mom Engle's words on to you: "You can't go on doubting whether you know Christ or not. You don't mess with eternity." As usual, she was right.

Exchanging Eternity

ROMANS 8:16-39

EAT UP

Because we've been trained by our culture to live by feelings, we often approach the Lord in the same way. We even consult our own emotions to determine whether we believe God's Word is true. When people carry doubts about their relationship to God, it is nearly always because they are substituting feelings for faith.

"The Spirit Himself testifies together with our spirit that we are God's children" (Romans 8:16).

Paul writes that "the Spirit Himself testifies together with our spirit that we are God's children." That doesn't mean the "testifying together with our spirit" is an emotional confirmation. Like so many other things, we can actively choose, rather than feel, the confirmation of God's Spirit. Many times, that confirmation comes from the Spirit through the Word of God.

How much time do you spend just "feeding" on the Scriptures? Think of the Bible as an enormous banquet table of the finest and freshest fruits, vegetables, cheeses, meats, and desserts, and you are the only person in the room. You are free to graze—taking some of this, some of that, and savoring it all. By spending time at that table, you take in nourishment that will sustain you and build your strength in the right way.

There are literally thousands of promises within the pages of your Bible. For example, Hebrews 13:5-6 declares: **"... He Himself has said, 'I will never leave you or forsake you.' Therefore, we may boldly say: 'The Lord is my helper; I will not be afraid. What can man do to me?'"**

If you continually "feast" on words like that, you will find your spirit nourished to health and maturity. You will also find your spirit converging with God's Spirit. In those words, brought to life by the Holy Spirit, is the deep and profound assurance of God's Fatherhood and eternal reliability.

"And if children, also heirs—heirs of God and coheirs with Christ—seeing that we suffer with Him so that we may also be glorified with Him" (Romans 8:17).

THAT'S WHAT YOU GET

When my mom died, she left me an inheritance. I couldn't touch it, however, until I was 18 years old. That delay was a good thing—what would an 11-year-old kid do with money? My inheritance was a trust fund that was established to help pay for my college education. Since I met my wife in college, that inheritance also opened the door to blessings beyond my wildest dreams.

So what does our inheritance in God look like?

First off, it's so large that it will (or should) overwhelm you. In fact, God has a way of hiding the full truth of it until we are mature enough to handle it. Until we can use it with wisdom, our inheritance will remain in a "trust." Like so many other elements of life with Christ, our understanding of our inheritance will grow as our walk with Him becomes deeper. Through that deepening, we will, over time, come to appreciate the fullness of what God has for us. For now, we can glean some information from those who have walked before us.

Psalm 2:7-8 contains a prophetic song of the Father God's word to His Son: **"I will declare the LORD's decree: He said to Me, 'You are My Son; today I have become Your Father. Ask of Me, and I will make the nations Your inheritance and the ends of the earth Your possession.'"**

Hebrews 1:2 then refers to **"His Son, whom He has appointed heir of all things."**

So our inheritance (as "co-heirs" with Jesus) is the whole earth. Think about it: The nations of the earth belong to God, and He gives them as an inheritance to His Son and His Son's fellow-heirs. The nations do not belong to Satan or any of the visible power centers of politics, religion, big business, or multi-national conglomerates. They belong to God—and we get to share in that.

As co-heirs with Christ, we can participate in the increase of God's government— His kingdom—in the earth. Revelation 11:15 declares that **"the kingdom of the world has become the kingdom of our Lord, and of His Messiah, and He will reign forever and ever!"**

But God's kingdom is not a collection of smaller kingdoms. Becoming a co-heir with Christ is not some kind of "career move." He will not allow little "sheikdoms" of private enrichment, political power, and sensual indulgence. In fact, the qualification for this inheritance is based on our identification with the suffering and death of Christ. Just as Christ suffered and died, we are called to suffer and die to ourselves.

Such a costly inheritance will not come to those who have not embraced the cross. God's kingdom is not our own, for our good alone. Jesus announced that **"the kingdom of God has come near" (Mark 1:14)**. He came to usher in a new reign that would spread throughout the earth. Many of the unfathomable and very real problems of the earth—hunger, disease, racism, cruelty, war—will disappear only as His righteous reign heals and beautifies lands and nations. Yet we cannot sit around waiting for that to happen one day. As co-heirs we become part of it.

The kingdom of God has come near, and if we identify with Christ in His death, burial, and resurrection, then we have a responsibility to participate with Him in the kingdom-creation process.

"For I consider that the sufferings of this present time are not worth comparing with the glory that is going to be revealed to us" (Romans 8:18).

Why did Paul say "suffering"? We will not move into our inheritance without suffering in our time. Suffering takes our selves, our hopes, our dreams, and all our preferences to the cross. None of us is qualified in our present state to "rule and reign with Him." By embracing suffering, we are allowing God to wean us from those things that compete for our allegiance and affection. When we pass through the "sufferings of this present age," however, we will touch a glory that will surpass any memories of the pain we once had to endure. No comparison.

We cannot afford to get caught up in what's temporary and superficial in this world. Walking with Christ is as "counterculture" as we can possibly live. To walk with Christ is to live by His claims and His kingdom. It's a rejection of the values and standards of our culture and our world. Now *that* is countercultural.

Walking with Jesus is a commitment to a new way of living. It is a commitment to His kingdom and His causes. In light of that, we must continue to develop an eternal mind-set. There is more to life than what happens on planet earth.

One day we will see the One we serve in all His glory and universal authority. Heaven is a real place, and one day because of Christ, we will be there with Him forever. Our eternal inheritance is surely more than we can fathom. Yet it does not begin "one day when"; it starts now in this life you have been given.

> What value is there in dwelling on the reality of heaven? How can we balance that with the reality of life in the here and now?

Session 6 **The Exchange**

How does a kingdom mind-set cause you to view the world around you? How does it change the way you live?

FREE AT LAST

One of the most beautiful places on earth is Montana's Glacier National Park. The white-capped mountain tops pierce right through the powder blue sky. Standing in that panoramic splendor, you can smell the spice of Pine, Blue Spruce, and Douglas fir trees. The trickling of water moving over rocks in its tumble toward the basin of the valley completes this sensory experience. Bears and other wildlife roam freely. The salmon jump in the streams as they move up to the headwaters. You can see the craftsmanship of God all over that majestic place.

Places like Glacier National Park seem to be oases in a world filled with tragedy and pain. Wars, crime, terrorism, hunger, disease, and so many other catastrophes mar the transcendent glory of God's creation.

"For the creation eagerly waits with anticipation for God's sons to be revealed. For the creation was subjected to futility—not willingly, but because of Him who subjected it—in the hope that the creation itself will also be set free from the bondage of corruption into the glorious freedom of God's children" (Romans 8:19-21).

I wrote earlier about the cycle of futility in the earth resulting from Adam and Eve's sin. Thankfully, that futility is not total and is not forever. The glory of God's reign is setting creation free from that futile pattern. Nature itself longs for God to redeem the universe.

"There is no element," John Calvin wrote, "and no part of the world which, being touched … with a sense of its present misery, does not intensely hope for a resurrection."[19]

What looks like chaos and catastrophe sounds very different if we filter it through a spiritual lens. The earth itself groans for its Creator-God to wipe out the residue of sin and establish His eternal kingdom. Creation also waits in anticipation to see God's children (that would be you and me) glorified and whole.

And the planet is being set free. Things that appear as disasters to us—tsunamis, earthquakes, hurricanes—are signs of our need for God. They are signs that God is still working on and in this planet. God cares about earth and has a better ecological plan than any environmental group ever dreamed: total restoration.

The Second Law of Thermodynamics (the law of entropy, or certain diminishing of energy) tells us that the universe is heading toward destruction and chaos. The Bible teaches that it was humanity's sin that created murder, hate, and even corrupted nature itself. Could there be a connection between entropy and sin?

Nothing caught God by surprise; He knew the path of humanity's rebellion. But in His larger kindness and generosity, He also provided redemption for the earth itself. Where sin abounds, grace does more abound. Because Jesus is the King of a righteous kingdom, we—and even the earth itself—are looking forward to God's reversal of the law of entropy.

A PAINFUL GAIN

I will never forget the day that Elizabeth, our firstborn, came into the world. My wife, Valerie, was in labor for almost twenty-four hours. We had waited for nine months up to that day, yet the real suffering had just begun for Valerie (and for me having to watch her). Despite all of the pain of childbirth, the joy of seeing Elizabeth come into the world far outweighed all of the hardship.

"For we know that the whole creation has been groaning together with labor pains until now. And not only that, but we ourselves who have the Spirit as the firstfruits—we also groan within ourselves, eagerly waiting for adoption, the redemption of our bodies. Now in this hope we were saved, yet hope that is seen is not hope, because who hopes for what he sees? But if we hope for what we do not see, we eagerly wait for it with patience" (Romans 8:22-25).

I believe all of creation—even people who haven't yet met their Redeemer—is groaning in labor pains. Those who are not in Christ don't know the reason for their groaning, but they can feel the emptiness of a life without God. Everyone in all creation struggles with the effects of sin in the earth, sensing that something is wrong.

Do you believe a day is coming when all of God's children will see Jesus reestablish His kingdom on earth? I certainly do. In that day, all humanity will suddenly see clearly. The Bible says, **"All the ends of the earth will remember and turn to the LORD. All the families of the nations will worship before You" (Psalm 22:27)**. Those who do not know Him now will "suddenly remember." But they will not experience the blessings of His kingdom.

Jesus Christ will be the light of world. He will right every wrong, judge the wicked and the dead, and we will see a new heaven coming down to earth (Revelation 21:1). Hopes, even those unspoken, will be fulfilled.

But those of us in the Spirit have access now to this future glory. Not only that, but the Spirit currently lives is in us and comforts us through the pain of entropy.

In light of this incredible truth, how do you think we should respond to the labor pains and trials that we experience in this life? All of our struggles mean something. God is preparing us for the future. Honestly, I do not understand all of the "why's" and "how's," but I know that God is sovereign.

If we knew how to interpret the sounds, sights, and events happening on earth, I think we would realize that the whole creation is speaking of the need for and ongoing process of redemption. The people of the earth are joining in that chorus.

PRAY FOR ME

"In the same way the Spirit also joins to help in our weakness, because we do not know what to pray for as we should, but the Spirit Himself intercedes for us with unspoken groanings. And He who searches the hearts knows the Spirit's mind-set, because He intercedes for the saints according to the will of God" (Romans 8:26-27).

In times of groaning like these, we often are too weak or confused to know how to pray. The Holy Spirit picks up where our shortsightedness leaves off. As our "advocate," the Spirit looks out for us even when we do not look out for ourselves. When life roars over and around us, the Spirit who lives in our hearts is never overwhelmed. He stays with us and carries us through.

What a great and mighty God we serve and worship. He is always near us. Even when present times and circumstances seem dark, the future is bright for those who put their hope in Christ. We are never alone.

The Spirit who is within you is whispering the truth of that new world. Listen closely, and you can hear the song of hope through the despair.

How do these verses change your perspective on world events?

What are the unspoken groanings you don't know how to pray for?

A BIGGER VIEW

Now we arrive at some of the most *heaven-invading-earth* words in the entire Bible.

"We know that all things work together for the good of those who love God: those who are called according to His purpose" (Romans 8:28).

Our great Father God sees all things at once. He is not subject to time and space. He never has to wonder how things will turn out; He sees all things complete. He does not pace around Heaven, wringing His hands about the condition of the earth or even your life. He has already decided that He is going to work everything out for your good.

Because you live in time and space, you will, of course, travel through experiences that do not seem good at the moment. In fact, they may distress and terrify you. But hold on because you are caught in the grip of the majestic Creator and King of the universe.

WHAT'S THE PLAN?

Consider the story of Joseph as told in Genesis 37–50. Joseph was his father's favorite son, and his brothers hated him for it. They kidnapped him, beat him up, and sold him to a band of traders. They dipped his clothes in blood so they could deceive their father into believing that Joseph had been killed by wild animals. The band of traders took him to Egypt and sold him into slavery. Potiphar, a powerful and prominent official in Pharaoh's government, bought Joseph.

The situation was unjust, yet Joseph's love for God remained pure, and he was promoted him to be Potiphar's top servant. But Joseph's story was about to become worse. After a time, Potiphar's wife tried to seduce Joseph. One day she made sexual advances toward him. In the struggle to get away from her, she tore off a piece of his clothing. She used that fabric to falsely accuse Joseph of attempted rape. Naturally, Potiphar threw Joseph in prison, where he remained for several years.

If you freeze-framed the story right there, you might begin to think that God doesn't care. What kind of God allows those who love Him so passionately and purely to suffer outrageous injustice? Would Joseph have been justified in blowing off the whole God idea? But you have to read the whole story to get an accurate perspective.

After the young Hebrew spent years in prison, God brought Joseph to King Pharaoh's attention. The king was troubled by weird dreams, and Joseph was the only one who could interpret them.

In one of the dreams, Joseph saw a famine coming to Egypt. Because Pharaoh was so impressed, he appointed Joseph second-in-command of Egypt. He became the equivalent of prime minister. With his new position, Joseph assumed responsibility for averting the famine. Because of his wisdom, the nation did not suffer loss during those days of hunger and suffering. In fact, all the surrounding countries became dependent on Egypt for food. One day a group from Canaan appeared before Joseph to buy supplies. When Joseph saw them, he recognized them immediately as his brothers, the same guys who had sold him to the band of traders years earlier.

Joseph allowed his family to buy food and eventually revealed his true identity. (Wouldn't you like to have seen their faces?) He could have had his brothers killed, but instead he forgave them, replenished their food supply, and saved their lives.

Do you realize that if God had intervened to save Joseph from injustice and slavery, Egyptian civilization might have collapsed? Even the land that eventually became Israel would have been devastated by the famine. Many nations would have suffered great loss; thousands of people would have starved.

Not only that, but God used Joseph to preserve the lineage that delivered the Messiah, Jesus, thousands of years later.

Joseph's own summary of the story showed that he understood the higher ways of God. He told his brothers, **"You planned evil against me; God planned it for good to bring about the present result—the survival of many people" (Genesis 50:19-20).**

God does cause "all things to work together for good." I am amazed that despite the injustice, suffering, and rejection, Joseph trusted in God's sovereignty. Somehow God used all of the hardship of Joseph's journey to preserve Israel and the rest of the world.

We see the same pattern in the life of Christ—great suffering and injustice leveraged great salvation. Maybe, just maybe, God knows what He is doing in your life too. Do you think you can trust Him with your journey?

GLORY ROAD

God doesn't leave us alone. He is constantly working in our lives and all around us. Even when we do stupid things, God continues working through us. If you are His child, there is nothing that can happen to you that God cannot use for good. His purposes for you cannot be stopped.

"For those He foreknew He also predestined to be conformed to the image of His Son, so that He would be the firstborn among many brothers. And those He predestined, He also called; and those He called, He also justified; and those He justified, He also glorified" (Romans 8:29-30).

Trust me: God will do whatever it takes to make us more like His Son. The great, intricate tapestry of His purpose has many threads. He is going to finish that tapestry, including that part with your name on it, because He is faithful (Philippians 1:6).

From His eternal vantage point, God sees all of time in one glimpse.

Like Joseph, Daniel, Ruth, Abraham, Peter, Paul, and so many others throughout history, we can be confident of the glory that exceeds our human imagination. God has planned incredible things for His people from the beginning of time.

HELP, WE NEED SOMEBODY

Luke told a beautiful story of how Jesus, the Son of God, interacted with humanity: **"Just as He neared the gate of the town, a dead man was being carried out. He was his mother's only son, and she was a widow. A large crowd from the city was also with her. When the Lord saw her, He had compassion on her and said, 'Don't cry.' Then He came up and touched the open coffin, and the pallbearers stopped. And He said, 'Young man, I tell you, get up!'" (Luke 7:12-16).**

Think about it: People saw this person—God—emotionally moved by the pathos of a human situation. More than that, God raised the mother's son from the dead and gave the boy back to her. He didn't even try to recruit the kid into His movement. These ordinary, everyday people watched that incredible scene and concluded in profound fashion: *"God has come to help."*

"What then are we to say about these things? If God is for us, who is against us? He did not even spare His own Son, but offered Him up for us all; how will He not also with Him grant us everything?" (Romans 8:31-32).

THE FATHER I NEVER HAD

Growing up without a dad was indescribably difficult. I always wanted someone to be committed to me, take up for me, protect me, and help me meet my potential. I wanted someone to care.

Session 6 **The Exchange**

Without that, I began to live in a cycle of rejection—some real, some self-inflicted. I developed a "reject them before they reject me" complex. The cycle got worse, and I started to feel like the whole world was against me. Eventually I came to believe that God was against me as well.

Even as I began in ministry, I still carried around the idea that even though God was with me, He was constantly waiting for the chance to punish me because of His disappointment. When something would go wrong, I would conclude that I had failed to live up to my Father's expectations, and He had sent judgment.

I wrote a song called "The Father I Never Had." Some of the lyrics tell the story of that cycle:

> … *Daddy left without a trace*
> *I never even saw his face*
> *Was I to blame?*
> *I still feel the pain*
> *Of a heart shattered like glass*
> *That cut my soul to pieces*
> *I never thought I'd love again*

Then, as I dove further into the truth about God, I started to see that the great and mighty God of the universe was for me. I saw the same thing the people saw when Jesus raised the boy from the dead: God is for His people; He is for me, *Joel Engle*. At that point, I could finish the lyrics of the song:

> *Until I met you, Jesus*
> *You're the Father I never had*

All of a sudden, my entire reason for living changed. It no longer mattered that I struggled with things. *God is for me.* When I got that established in my heart, it didn't matter that other kids were more popular than I, that I was financially unstable, or that I struggled with my weight. *God is for me.* This revelation—one of the most powerful truths any Christian can comprehend—changed everything for me.

DON'T MESS WITH THIS

I played football in junior high. It was not the brightest idea I ever had; when I was in the seventh grade, I weighed about 100 pounds. I had a tough attitude and a big mouth, but my body could just never get on the same page with my attitude. My mouth kept writing checks that my scrawny body couldn't cash.

One day Tommy Remis and some of his buddies decided to use me as a tackling dummy. His accomplices held my arms as Tommy (in football pads) began running as hard as he could toward me. My insides turned to liquid fear as this refrigerator-sized bully advanced at breakneck speed. Moments before impact, James Bell, the toughest guy in the whole school, tackled Tommy Remis.

James looked down at Tommy, stunned and coughing on the ground, and said, "If you mess with Joel you mess with me." It sounded as though God Himself had growled the warning. I carry that memory as a picture of the way God looks at us. He takes up for His children. God looks at our enemy, who wants to kill us, and roars, "If you mess with this one, you mess with Me!"

IN YOUR DEFENSE

"Who can bring an accusation against God's elect? God is the One who justifies. Who is the one who condemns? Christ Jesus is the One who died, but even more, has been raised. He also is at the right hand of God and intercedes for us" (Romans 8:33-34).

The Bible calls Satan "the accuser" (Revelation 12:10). Since he has been defeated, he has no authority over people. So he is now reduced to hurling accusations at us.

Imagine a courtroom scene. Satan slinks in a chair on the front row and continually spews accusations about the children of God. All too often our response to those accusations is to acknowledge their truth and hang our heads in shame.

Eleanor Roosevelt once spoke a profound spiritual truth when she said, "No one can make you feel inferior without your permission." The devil wages a war of discouragement, fear, and hopelessness against God's loved ones. But the only way that campaign of accusation can ever work is with our permission. So when Satan wins, it is because people choose to accept and agree with his charges.

If you listen carefully, however, you will hear clearly that Satan's voice is not the only one in the courtroom. There is a greater, deeper, and more powerful one speaking. That superior Voice is also speaking on our behalf.

Christ now stands in that courtroom as our defender. In fact, we don't even have to go to court. He stands there in our place, defending us with the truth that we are free because of Him. We don't have to listen to the enemy any longer. He is defeated. He only wins if we allow him to.

Like any good lawyer, our advocate has brought evidence of His own about our accuser: **"He was a murderer from the beginning, not holding to the truth, for there is no truth in him. When he lies, he speaks his native language, for he is a liar and the father of lies" (John 8:44).**

It's time to stop living by your instincts and feelings and take God at His Word. You are free from sin and condemnation. Forever.

Our confidence is not in our biblical knowledge or our own goodness. Our confidence is placed in what Jesus did for us on the cross. His Redemption must be the place where we go when Satan begins to accuse us of "not being worthy."

If God is for us, who can be against us?

Do you believe that God is not just with you, but *for* you?

What circumstances in your life threaten to make you doubt God's "for-ness"?

I'VE GOT SOMETHING TO SAY

We live in an age of uncertainty, pessimism, and cynicism. The threats of global terrorism, environmental disasters, global epidemics like AIDS, financial volatility, and other crises seem to daily terrorize people and nations.

Yet the Psalmist tells us that God surveys all the uproar, vanity, sin, and rebellion on earth, and He is not intimidated by, confused about, or uncertain regarding any condition on earth. He is not fearful or disturbed. The great Creator of the universe is at peace.

Everyone is positioned in their time and place on earth for a reason. Whether they ever perceived it or not, God chose for them to be born in that historical moment and location. For those who would hear it, a call sounded out of heaven for them to be His light in troubled times.

Every time in history has been troubled. Everyone who ever lived has existed under threat of destruction. No time of history has been "safe." Yet we all have an opportunity to walk through our place and times as ambassadors—representatives—of heaven.

You have been sent by the King Himself to announce a new way—a better way—of living. We have the great opportunity to pull prisoners from their chains into the freedom in the kingdom of the Son of God.

We have the honor of living as heralds of "all things new" (Revelation 21:1–5).

HEY, FOCUS!

"Who shall separate us from the love of Christ? Can affliction or anguish or persecution or famine or nakedness or danger or sword? As it is written: 'Because of You we are being put to death all day long; we are counted as sheep to be slaughtered'" (Romans 8:35-36).

Despite their benign appearance, the power centers of our world have always been capable of great cruelty and inhumanity. Politics, religion, business, and other fronts of this present age will bare their true fangs when they are pressed into a corner. Many innocent people have been slaughtered like sheep when the political, religious, or economic interests were threatened.

In Romans 8: 36, Paul is essentially saying, "Stay focused." OK, so we're considered (by the power centers) as mere sheep to be slaughtered (as they march toward their objectives). It doesn't ultimately matter. Those threats are of no consequence because nothing and no one can ever separate us from the love of God through Christ. *Nothing.* Even the worst-case scenario cannot threaten us. Even if we are slaughtered, we still win.

Those who have exchanged their life for the life of Jesus Christ will be victorious no matter what this world throws at them.

REAL VICTORY

"No, in all these things we are more than victorious through Him who loved us" (Romans 8:37).

In an age of *American Idol*, lotteries, and celebrity poker, the whole idea of "winning" has been trivialized. If you want to know the real image of winning, consider this story:

In Sistine Chapel hangs Michelangelo's magnificent work *The Last Judgment*. Next to Christ's image in the painting is a man named Lawrence the Deacon.

Session 6 **The Exchange**

This ancient saint was a man who deeply loved Christ and lived an exchanged life. During a time of great distress in the Roman Empire, many Roman citizens were going hungry. Lawrence the Deacon, who was also a treasurer in the Roman church, was known for saving many lives through his care for the poor.

In 257 A.D., the Emperor Valerian issued an edict to ban all Christian gatherings and confiscate all church property. A year later, the Emperor ordered the arrest of Lawrence. Once in custody, he was offered his freedom if he would only surrender the wealth of the church to the state. Surprisingly, Lawrence agreed.

He said that it would take him three days to round up all of the treasury. On the third day, Lawrence reported to the Roman prefect. Instead of money, he brought hundreds of widows, orphans, poor believers and the elderly members of the church. He announced to the Roman prefect, "These are the treasures of the Church."

On August 10 in the year 258 A.D., Lawrence the Deacon was executed by being roasted on a gridiron. Before his death, he was unusually peaceful. As he was dying, he said to his executioners, "You may turn me over; I am done on this side." He died moments later.

Lawrence the Deacon understood that "in all these things," even in the face of a painful and brutal death, he was victorious in Christ. It is significant and revealing that he could face that with a fine sense of humor. That is what winning looks like.

LET LOVE RULE

"For I am persuaded that neither death nor life, not angels nor rulers, nor things present, nor things to come, nor powers, nor height, nor depth, nor any other created thing will have the power to separate us from the love of God that is in Christ Jesus our Lord!" (Romans 8:38–39).

The Message paraphrases Romans 8:38-39 this way: **"I'm absolutely convinced that nothing—nothing living or dead, angelic or demonic, today or tomorrow, high or low, thinkable or unthinkable—absolutely nothing can between us and God's love that is in Christ Jesus our Lord."**

This statement by Paul is one of the most sweeping views of truth contained in the Bible. *"Nothing* can get between us and God's love … ." You could live a thousand years, but you would never encounter anything on earth that could get between you and the deep and abiding love of our Father.

Why would we ever think that anything we have encountered represents a "special case"?

The truths of God's Word contained in the sixth, seventh, and eight chapters of Romans are irrefutable and immutable. They are true in all places and seasons and centuries of life on planet earth.

The fact is, God loves us completely, consistently and eternally. Nothing can ever come between God's love for the world and for His people. He loves you more than you can ever know.

The old song "The Love of God" tells it very well:

> Could we with ink the ocean fill
> And were the skies of parchment made,
> Were every stalk on earth a quill
> And every man a scribe by trade,
> To write the love of God above
> Would drain the ocean dry,
> Nor could the scroll contain the whole
> Though stretched from sky to sky.

From the inexhaustible well of God's affection came the Son to pay the debt we owed, and He invites us to exchange that holy life for ours. He desires a full, dynamic, joyful and never-ending relationship with those who have accepted that invitation.

His life awaits. Go ahead: Accept. Die. Live. Exchange.

🛒✓ Take Away

☐ Spend some time remembering a funeral you attended recently. What was the dominant theme there? Journal your thoughts.
☐ Take a long walk outdoors with this thought in your mind: Creation groans in anticipation for the revelation of the children of God.
☐ Commit Romans 8:38-39 to memory.

"For I am persuaded that neither death nor life, nor angels nor rulers, nor things present, nor things to come, nor powers, nor height, nor depth, nor any other created thing will have the power to separate us from the love of God that is in Christ Jesus our Lord!"
—Romans 8:38-39

Session 6 **The Exchange**

Prayer

THEREFORE, let us desire nothing else,

Let us wish for nothing else,

Let nothing else please us and cause us delight,

Except our Creator and Redeemer and Savior, the one true God,

Who is the Fullness of Good, all good, every good,

The true and supreme good,

Who alone is Good, merciful, and gentle, delectable and sweet,

Who alone is holy and just and true, holy and right,

Who alone is kind, innocent, pure,

From Whom and through Whom and in Whom is all pardon,

All grace, all glory of all the penitent and the just,

Of all the blessed who rejoice together in heaven.

Therefore, let nothing hinder us, nothing separate us,

Or nothing come between us.

AUTHOR UNKNOWN

Notes

Session 6 **The Exchange**

Notes

GROUP CONTACT INFORMATION

Name _____ Number _____
Email _____

Name _____ Number _____
Email _____

Name _____ Number _____
Email _____

Name _____ Number _____
Email _____

Name _____ Number _____
Email _____

Name _____ Number _____
Email _____

Name _____ Number _____
Email _____

Name _____ Number _____
Email _____

Name _____ Number _____
Email _____

Name _____ Number _____
Email _____

Name _____ Number _____

Email _____

Name _____ Number _____

Email _____

Name _____ Number _____

Email _____

Name _____ Number _____

Email _____

Name _____ Number _____

Email _____

Name _____ Number _____

Email _____

Name _____ Number _____

Email _____

Name _____ Number _____

Email _____

Name _____ Number _____

Email _____

Name _____ Number _____

Email _____

What is Threads?

WE ARE A COMMUNITY OF PEOPLE WHO ARE PIECING THE CHRISTIAN LIFE TOGETHER, ONE EXPERIENCE AT A TIME.

We're rooted in Romans 12 and Colossians 3. We're serious about worshipping God with our lives. We want to understand the grace Jesus extended to us on the cross and act on it. We want community, need to worship, and aren't willing to sit on our hands when the world needs help. We want to grow. We crave Bible study that raises questions, makes us think, and causes us to own our faith. We're interested in friendships that are as strong as family ties — the kind of relationships that transform individuals into communities.

Our Bible studies are designed specifically for you, featuring flexible formats with engaging video, audio, and music. These discussion-driven studies intentionally foster group and individual connections and encourage practical application of Scripture. You'll find topical articles, staff and author blogs, podcasts, and lots of other great resources at:

threads by LifeWay

THREADSMEDIA.COM

STOP BY TO JOIN OUR ONLINE COMMUNITY AND COME BY TO VISIT OFTEN!

THE TOUGH SAYINGS OF JESUS
by Michael Kelley

This study explores four statements Jesus made that are difficult to grasp. Delving into the historical and cultural contexts of these Scriptures, the study focuses on sparking discussion and providing fresh insight, not pat answers. It will encourage you to embrace your doubts, and process through them, so that your faith can become deeper and stronger.

Michael Kelley is a writer and traveling communicator who speaks to students and young adults throughout the United States. Passionate about effectively communicating the fullness of the good news of Jesus, Michael previously served as the principle teacher for Refuge, a weekly worship event for young adults in Nashville, Tennessee. Visit him at www.michaelkelleyonline.com.

IN TRANSIT
WHAT DO YOU DO WITH YOUR WAIT?
by Mike Harder

Do you often feel that you're waiting for real life to begin? This study introduces you to three truths about waiting as it traces the lives of David, Jesus, and Joseph — all promised great things and all of whom waited, sometimes painfully, to see God's promises come to pass. You'll discover that waiting without purpose can lead to loneliness and doubting God, but purposeful waiting brings a sense of fulfillment and an awareness of God's timing and faithfulness.

Mike Harder is a regular face and speaker at The Loop in Memphis, Tennessee, a weekly Bible study for young adults. He also serves on the staff of Highpoint Church overseeing the church's connection ministry. Find him at www.mikeharderministries.com.

GET UNCOMFORTABLE
SERVE THE POOR. STOP INJUSTICE.
CHANGE THE WORLD ... IN JESUS' NAME
by Todd Phillips

Phillips guides you to understand how your faith in Christ and concern for the poor go hand-in-hand. As he examines God's character and perspective regarding poverty and injustice, he offers an understanding of what God calls you to do, along with practical ways to impact culture by caring for "the least of these."

Todd Phillips is the teaching pastor of Frontline, the young adult ministry of McLean Bible Church near Washington D.C. His passions are teaching the people of God and sharing the Gospel with those who aren't yet Christians. He is the author of CPR: Reviving a Flat-lined Generation.

THE TOUGH SAYINGS OF JESUS

Michael Kelley

Table of Contents

Introduction: Redefining Jesus?

What images come to your mind when you hear or see the name Jesus?

We come from different backgrounds, knowledge bases, and experiences. All those things influence our perceptions, even our perceptions of the same Scriptures we've read about whom Jesus is.

The Bible refers to Jesus as the Alpha and Omega, the Lamb slain before the foundation of the world, and the Savior of the world. In the first chapter of John, He is the Word that was with God, and yet was God, from the beginning. The gospels (Matthew, Mark, Luke, and John) say He is the Son, the Shepherd, and Seeker of the lost. But how do those descriptions play out in our understanding? We may use the same terms, but until we talk it through, we can't be sure if our understanding of those words really mesh.

That's why it's good for us to look at Scripture together. According to the Bible, Jesus has existed throughout history, whether as the mysterious fourth figure in the fiery furnace story of the Old Testament book of Daniel, or as the seemingly blasphemous miracle worker of the New Testament gospels. The image of the person may change, but the essence of who He is remains the same. It is that essence that we will dive into during this study.

THROUGH A NEW LENS

We also see Jesus through different lenses in different seasons of our lives. C.S. Lewis puts great words to this in his Chronicles of Narnia series. The novels present a Christ-figure in the form of a lion named Aslan in a country called Narnia. At one point in the stories, the youngest character, Lucy, returns to Narnia after some time away. She tells Aslan that he is bigger than when she left. Aslan wisely explains that he seems bigger to her, not because he has grown, but because *she* has: "Every year you grow, you will find me bigger." And so it is with our view of Jesus. Our experiences don't change who He is, but they do give us a different vantage point as we, with the guidance of the Holy Spirit, revisit what we understand about Him.

If you grew up going to church, your understanding of Jesus may have been built with macaroni art and felt board stories. The pictures you saw might have portrayed a generous man with a welcoming smile full of love and compassion. We were probably taught that Jesus loved us and wanted to live inside of us. In this way, many of us began our relationship with Him.

For some, though, the relationship stayed within the confines of that scenario. The relationship did not grow as we grew. Our knowledge of Him remained very simple while our lives became increasingly complex. For those of us, it's very possible that this trimmed-down version of the Son of God has been bursting at the seams to escape the small understanding our minds and hearts have created for Him.

It's very possible that this trimmed-down version of the Son of God has been bursting at the seams to escape the small understanding our minds and hearts have created for Him.

THE RULE OF EXPANSION

Relationships are dynamic. They are a give-and-take process as time goes on; years after beginning a relationship with someone, we look back at the early days and wonder if we really knew the person at all back then. Why should our relationship with Christ be any different?

As wonderful as a growing relationship with a living God may sound and seem, there is an uncomfortable element to the continual reformation it requires. As we allow Jesus to burst through the macaroni frame and leap off the felt board, we may not always be comfortable. We may not be so sure we knew Jesus at all back then. Some parts of His ministry may not only be difficult to understand, but downright troubling.

Let's navigate these waters, even if they test our comfort zones. We cannot escape the fact that we don't completely understand everything Jesus said. But, if we are to be in an authentic, growing relationship with Him, we need to explore what we don't understand. Have you avoided certain passages of the Bible because you didn't understand them or they didn't jive with the Jesus you've come to accept? Consider the following: Did Jesus look down on non-Jews? Was He a racist? Did He dishonor His family and ask His followers to do the same? Did Jesus teach about grace through faith, like the rest of the New Testament, or was He more about us proving our love for Him through our actions? These are some of the questions we'll explore in this study.

Hopefully, this experience will help us to face head-on what Scripture teaches — and doesn't teach — about Jesus' life and ministry. If we can revisit what the Bible says, then we can compare what we understand (or misunderstand) the facts to mean. Many of us have staked our faith on Christ. It is up to us, then, to revisit from time to time what we have put our faith in and whether what we've experienced in life has given us a greater ability to understand the truth about Jesus.

THE BEAUTY IN DOUBT
Sometimes an over-simplified view of faith can leave us with the idea that we should shy away from the tough questions out of fear that our faith could be injured. Before we proceed with the study, let's define faith.

In some theological vocabularies, faith is represented as "the absence of doubt." With that definition, the measure of how much faith we have is determined by how little doubt accompanies it.

But is there really anything in our lives that doesn't contain a certain measure of doubt or at least questioning? Unfortunately, an over-simplified definition of faith doesn't leave room for questions, and so we end up living with closeted doubt that only shows its face during the most grim and troubling times in our lives.

There is a more realistic — and more authentic — way to approach faith and doubt. Our definition of faith should be more than the absence of doubt; instead, doubt can be an essential element to the process of faith. We have faith in something bigger than our doubts and questions. We don't have to fear them. If we can push hard into our questions instead of hiding them, we trust God to be bigger. And He is. God is big enough to receive us, doubt and all. Doubts and questions do not counter faith; instead, they should push us deeper.

Let's embrace authentic faith. Let's look at all that we know about Christ, even the parts we can't completely figure out. Let's let Him speak to us through what the Bible teaches, even if we don't completely understand. Even when, as in the Scripture for Session 1, it seems He tells a self-righteous young man that the key to salvation is not faith at all—but works ...

Listen to the audio file "Conflict Insulation." It will come via email from your group leader. Think about the following questions as you listen and come to your group's first study lesson ready to discuss your thoughts.

- How does our avoidance of conflict relate to our faith?
- How do we try to insulate our faith in a "comfortable fortress of security?"
- How does navigating through doubt actually strengthen your faith?

END NOTES

1 R. C. Sproul, *Romans* (Scotland: Christian Focus Publications Lted, 1994), 112.

2 Bill Gillham, *Lifetime Guarantee* (Eugene, Harvest House Publishers, 1993), 18.

3 Francis Schaeffer, *True Spirituality* (Wheaton: Tyndale House Publishers, 1971), 17.

4 F.F. Bruce, *The Epistle of Paul to the Romans* (Grand Rapids: The Tyndale Press, 1963), 139.

5 Eugene H. Peterson, *A Long Obedience in the Same Direction: Discipleship in an Instant Society* (Ontario: Varsity Press, 1980), 83.

6 Kenneth S. Wuest, *Wuest's Word Studies* (Grand Rapids: Wm. B. Eerdmans Publishing Company, 1966), 91,108.

7 Ray C. Stedman, *Choose Your Master*, www.raystedman.org/romans1/0014.html.

8 Kenneth S. Wuest, *Wuest's Word Studies* (Grand Rapids: Wm. B. Eerdmans Publishing Company, 1966), 110.

9 Francis Schaeffer, *True Spirituality* (Wheaton: Tyndale House Publishers, 1971), 87.

10 John Stott, *Life in Christ* (Grand Rapids: Baker Books, 1979), 41.

11 John MacArthur, *Freedom from Sin; Dead to the Law*, www.biblebb.com/files/mac/sg45-50.htm.

12 John MacArthur, *Freedom from Sin; Dead to the Law*, www.biblebb.com/files/mac/sd45-52.htm.

13 Steven McVey, *Grace Rules* (Eugene: Harvest House Publishers), 65.

14 Joseph Girzone, *A Portrait of Jesus* (New York: Random House, 1998), 13.

15 Martin Luther, *Commentary on Galatians* (Grand Rapids: Fleming H. Revell), 381.

16 John MacArthur, *The Believer and Indwelling Sin: Part 1*, www.biblebb.com/files/mac/sg45-52.htm.

17 Ray C. Stedman, *No Condemnation*,www.raystedman.org/romans2/3518.html.

18 T. W. Hunt, *Mind of Christ* (Nashville: LifeWay Press, 1994), 22.

19 John Calvin, *The Epistles of Paul The Apostle to the Romans and to the Thessalonians* (Edinburgh: Oliver and Boyd, 1960), 172.